STUDIOPAPERBACK

J. CHRISTOPH BÜRKLE

Hans Scharoun

Artemis

Zurich · Munich · London

All rights reserved; no part of this publication may be
reproduced, stored in a retrieval system, or transmitted
in any form or by any means. electronic, mechanical,
photocopying, recording, or otherwise, without the
prior written permission of the Publishers.

© 1993 Artemis Verlags-AG, Zürich

English translation: Pamela Johnson

Printed in Germany
ISBN 1-874056-80-3 London
ISBN 3-7608-8140-8 Zurich

Contents

Hans Scharoun – From Expressionism to Organic Building 9
Scharoun as an avant-gardist: the Weissenhofsiedlung house 13
The development of an organic method 15
The planning of Berlin 19
Consolidating an organic architecture 22
Building for the community 24
The projects for the State Theatre in Kassel, the National Theatre in Mannheim
and the a-perspective as a design principle 26
The Zürich Schauspielhaus project and the Wolfsburg Municipal Theatre 31
Scharoun's legacy: the Kulturforum in Berlin 33

Buildings and Projects 39
Church in Bremerhaven 41
Watercolours for the 'Crystal Chain' 42
Theatre, social and cultural hall, Gelsenkirchen 44
Museum of Hygiene, Dresden 46
Friedrichstraße high-rise, Berlin 48
Commercial building at the Börsenhof, Königsberg, Prussia 50
Chicago Tribune Tower 52
Spa building in Bad Mergentheim 53
Bochum Town Hall 54
Cologne bridgehead 56
Trade fair and exhibition centre, Berlin 58
Transportable wooden house for the German Garden and Trades Exhibition,
Liegnitz, Silesia 60
Single-family house for the Werkbund Exhibition, 'Die Wohnung',
Stuttgart-Weissenhof 62
Road through the Ministry Gardens, Berlin 64
Extension of the Reichstag building, Berlin 66
Schlichtallee group of schools, Berlin-Lichtenberg 68
Apartment building on the Kaiserdamm, Berlin-Charlottenburg 70
Housing block for the Werkbund Exhibition, 'Wohnung und Werkraum', Breslau . . . 72
Apartment building on the Hohenzollerndamm, Berlin-Wilmersdorf 74
Siemensstadt *Siedlung*, site plan and housing, Berlin 76
Gustav-Adolf Memorial Church, Breslau-Zimpel 80
'The growing house' – a wooden house for the 'Sun, Light and Housing
for All' Exhibition (Sonne, Licht und Haus für alle), Berlin 82

Schminke House, Löbau, Saxony	84
Mattern House, Bornim, near Potsdam	88
Holiday houses for a hotel in Vitznau, Switzerland	90
House for Dr Baensch, Berlin-Spandau	92
Oskar Moll House, Berlin-Grunewald	94
Ferdinand Möller House, Zermützelsee near Altruppin, Brandenburg	96
Berlin plans – a first report	98
Exhibition pavilion for the Gerd Rosen Gallery, Berlin	100
Stuttgart Music Hall	102
Schminke House, Celle	104
Elementary school, Darmstadt	105
Heinrich Mendelsohn high-rise, Berlin-Charlottenburg	108
Kassel State Theatre	109
Mannheim National Theatre	112
'Romeo and Juliet' high-rises, Stuttgart-Zuffenhausen	114
Charlottenburg-Nord *Siedlung*, Berlin	116
Development plan for the Hansa district, Berlin-Tiergarten	118
Single-family houses for the Hansa district, Berlin-Tiergarten	120
Concert Hall for the Berlin Philharmonic Orchestra, Bundesallee, Berlin-Wilmersdorf, and Kemperplatz, Berlin-Tiergarten	121
The 'Geschwister Scholl' School, Lünen, Westphalia	128
Hauptstadt Berlin	130
Primary and Secondary School, Marl, Westphalia	132
'Salute' high-rise, Stuttgart	134
State Library for the Prussian Cultural Heritage Foundation, Berlin	136
German Embassy, Brasilia	140
Municipal Theatre, Wolfsburg	142
Chapel of St. John for the Community of Christ in Glockengarten, Bochum	145
Church of the Transfiguration of Christ, Berlin-Schöneberg	148
Protestant church and community centre, Wolfsburg-Rabenberg	150
German Maritime Museum, Bremerhaven	152
State Institute for Musical Research and Museum of Instruments, Berlin-Tiergarten	154
Chamber Music Hall for the Philharmonie, Berlin-Tiergarten	155
Appendix	**159**
Biography	161
Notes	165
Selected bibliography	168
List of works	170
Illustration credits	176

Hans Scharoun, music hall, watercolour, c. 1922.

Previous page: Hans Scharoun, c. 1927.

Hans Scharoun – From Expressionism to Organic Building

The selective way in which the history of Modernism has been written has meant that until recently it has been difficult to define the role of organic building in general, and the work of Hans Scharoun in particular, in 20th-century architecture. As we now know, architects such as Walter Gropius and Le Corbusier published only their Modernist work, suppressing early projects marked by compromises or regional influences to make it seem as if they had been born to the avant-garde. Their revisionist history was reinforced by authors such as Sigfried Giedion, whose influential *Space, Time and Architecture* effectively restricted the definition of Modernism to the 'International Style' and the German 'New Objectivity', excluding 'alternative' architects such as Scharoun, Mendelsohn and Bruno Taut.
Similarly, any objective analysis of the history of the New Architecture (*Neues Bauen*) is obscured by questions of style. Unlike other strands of Modernism, Expressionism is seldom thought of as having generated technically innovative architecture – an idea belied by works like Max Taut's Wissinger mausoleum in Stahnsdorf, near Berlin. Designed in 1921 and built between autumn 1922 and spring 1923, the mausoleum was one of the few executed Expressionist designs of the *Frühlicht* period. Its extremely slender framed concrete structure clearly impressed a young man working for Taut at the time – Mart Stam, who went on to promote the concrete frame as the progenitor of rational architecture. Stripped of 'Expressionist' elements, the twin-column concrete frame became for Stam the most important principle of design in the 1920s.
In the 1960s there was a revival of interest in Expressionism, and critics began to reassess the movement within the broader context of Modern architecture. Scharoun was seen as the representative of the defunct Expressionist period – and his Philharmonie as the belated fulfilment of its legacy. He was accused of capricious 'irrationalism',[1] and credited with the concept of 'expanded Functionalism', or 'organic Expressionism'.[2] Ultimately all of these descriptions were attempts to define what was to Scharoun the most important aspect of design: the relationship between space and form.
The first real opportunity to gain a closer understanding of Scharoun's work came with the publication in 1974 of a collection of documents edited by his long-time collaborator, Peter Pfankuch. But while the book is commendable, it is not comprehensive: the selection of material was made largely by Scharoun himself, and there are many omissions. Critics next turned their attention to assessing the relation of Scharoun's early utopian work to his later development and to defining a firm category for the impetus that give rise to the organic-functional and Expressionist work. This mystifying approach was encouraged by the fact that both Scharoun and Hugo Häring had always emphasized that the irrational character of the architecture was simply born of the design process. In this phase of assessment, Scharoun was deemed to be an 'expressive Functionalist'[3] – a curious synthesis of attribute. Indeed, it

Max Taut, Wissinger mausoleum, Berlin, 1921.

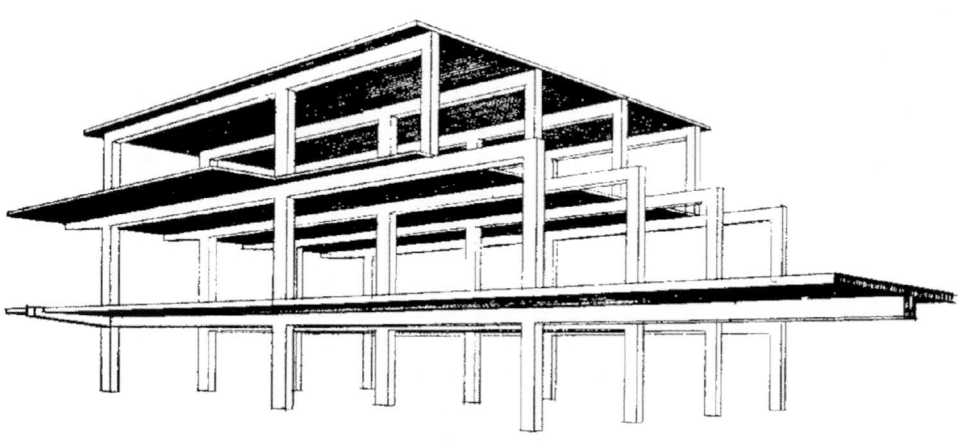

Mart Stam, residential building designed for future extension, 1924/25.

is astounding that Scharoun's reputation should have become so inextricably bound up with Expressionism when he tried all his life to avoid stylistic categorization.
At the time he was producing the work, the critics took a different view. In 1925, the year Scharoun left Insterburg for Breslau, Carl Claussen wrote: 'Scharoun has taken part in practically every competition he has been eligible for, but with comparatively little success. This

H. Scharoun, Friedrichstraße high-rise, Berlin, 1921.

may seem surprising, given the compelling, powerful ideas in each of his designs, but it can be explained by the fact that people with historicist sensibilities are put off by Scharoun's evident lack of knowledge of architectural history.'[4] Scharoun was mainly self-taught: he was enrolled at the Technische Hochschule in Berlin-Charlottenburg for only four terms, and even then was rarely seen in class. Claussen continued: because Scharoun 'is unversed in the forms of style, [he has to] approach each task afresh, and this gives his designs a breathtaking quality which even the most seasoned critic cannot resist.'[5] But even Scharoun did not work in a vacuum. His early drawings provide ample evidence both of his concern with relating buildings to their historical context, and of his familiarity with traditional stylistic forms. But naturally it was the flexibility and ease of Scharoun's work that caused such a stir in the early 1920s. Scharoun's greatest successes during this period were two competition designs – one for a high-rise at Friedrichstraße station in Berlin in 1921, the other for a commercial building and hotel at the Börsenhof in Königsberg in 1922.

The Friedrichstraße high-rise had a convincing concept, an unusual language of forms and an individualistic graphic presentation. It adhered closely to the brief and secured an award from the rather academic jury. It was described by Max Berg, the city planner of Breslau, as 'one of competition's most significant achievements, from an artistic point of view', its fantastic forms making it for him the 'most characteristic expression of the German concept of the high-rise in evidence in the competition.'[6] While the project was not widely publicized at the time, the Dutch magazine *Wendingen* gave a comprehensive account of it in a 1923 issue on high-rises.

Scharoun responded to the exposed nature of the three-sided plot with three different façades which stepped back in order to bring in light and allow for the proper distance from the surrounding buildings. While these urban-planning characteristics were determined by the site, the dynamic form was largely a product of a functional ordering of space. The stairwells formed glazed, vertical breaks in the façade, while the organization of the commercial spaces reinforced the horizontality of the lower part of the building. The transition at this point to a gothicized entrance was shown in 'radiant' views of the building at night, emblazoned with signage. Such night views were typical of the time; they symbolized the urban, metropolitan character of the project. The graphic devices of the single-point perspective and the lines denoting rays of light spelled out the link with the utopian 'people's houses'. Here, the references to Gothic architecture were of an indirect, rather ideal nature – a fashion also reflected in the Chicago Tribune Tower competition of 1922.

Although the design was not drawn up in full detail, it was precisely formulated in architectural and spatial terms. The plan initially appears complicated, as is often the case with Scharoun, but it shows, for the first time, completely resolved organizational sequences, junctions, and user-circulation.

In his Königsberg project, Scharoun went one step further. The plan dynamically follows a fixed line of movement which is only partly determined by the conditions of the site. The spaces are related to each other by function, and while the spatial divisions occasionally appear arbitrary, the width of the corridors corresponds organically to the amount of user traffic. The competition assessors had praise for the plan's 'vital note', but they criticized the evident 'influence of Finsterlin', the 'formal eclecticism in the design of the façades' and even 'the complete helplessness of the hotel exterior'.

The two competition designs brought Scharoun to the attention of an important critic and advocate of the New Architecture, Adolf Behne. In a letter to Scharoun, Behne acknowledged the quality of the principle behind his designs but said, unequivocally: 'A building should be organic, but never an "organism" in the sense of living nature – because it cannot be so! Dispense with all these notions of "organisms" – an organ is not a mouth, it does not suck, and so on – But don't get me wrong, Scharoun. Don't put any suns, moons or stars on your drawings. I was extremely annoyed to see that even the skies had to be part of the motion of your otherwise commendable – theatre. In my opinion, dynamic architecture must be unconditionally rational, as cold as the nose of a dog – otherwise it declines into drama.'[7] Correspondingly, when Behne came to illustrate his famous book *Der moderne Zweckbau*, he showed not the façade of Scharoun's Börsenhof project, but the plan, in which he saw an organic quality. By contrast, he showed the façades of Mart Stam's entry for the same competition, which corresponded more closely to the rationalist concept of a functional building.

Der moderne Zweckbau was one of the first texts to discuss organic architecture in depth. It looked explicitly at the works of Scharoun – and in doing so, hardly mentioned the term 'Expressionism'. Instead, Behne focused on the split in Modern architecture between the principle of collectivism and the principle of individualism. Rationalist Modernism, as practised by Hannes Meyer, Ernst May and Mart Stam, amongst others, was understood as the resolution of a collective task, which ultimately produced a typology based upon an objectified social task. But very early on, Behne realized that Scharoun's work was 'thoroughly individualistic'. He wrote: 'Despite its relationship to the street, etc., the structure is something individual, special; given this approach, the incorporation of elements of the site perhaps only further emphasizes the [building's] individual character.'[8] Behne then asked whether Scharoun's method of design would ever allow him to establish a 'typology'. The 'development of a typology', which in a broader sense meant also the development of a stylistic form, was a paradigm of Modernism, and the early Werkbund debates on this theme continued into the 1920s. It is clear that during this period Scharoun, like others, rejected typological formulas as the foundation of design, and saw function as being defined by the specific task in hand. In this he was closer to Louis Sullivan's dictum of 'form follows function' than to Rational Functionalism, in which function was the over-riding principle. Behne attempted, at least at this early stage, to combine the two strands and influence Scharoun with the logic of his theory. Scharoun in turn was grateful for what he termed the 'expansion of his mind' – which transmuted to greater formal coherence in his post-1923 designs. From that point, the plans no longer showed the curved lines of movement; the spatial divisions became more rational, sometimes even orthogonal. The façades reflected a search for a binding canon – a form that was whole, rather than an assemblage of many elements. This change in Scharoun's work brought with it a change in critical perception. In Gustav Adolf Platz's book *Die Baukunst der neuesten Zeit* (1927), Scharoun was described as representing the 'dynamic expression of function'.[9] His works were grouped as a matter of course with those of Erich Mendelsohn and linked with Mendelsohn's programme of 'functional dynamics'.

It is therefore not surprising that Mendelsohn should be one of the few influences to which Scharoun explicitly referred.[10] Scharoun adopted from Mendelsohn the key concept of 'functional dynamics', with its theoretical separation of rational and irrational. He also found that Mendelsohn's buildings, like his own, had a 'sensuous undercurrent' that went far beyond the application of the organic principle.

Scharoun as an avant-gardist: the Weissenhofsiedlung house
At the Weissenhofsiedlung Scharoun showed that he was not prepared to submit fully to the stringent dogma of Functionalism or the International Style, as it was later called. He was not on the original list of Weissenhof architects, but was asked to participate at a later stage, after his elevation from the provinces to the ranks of the avant-garde. The Weissenhof house is not only one of Scharoun's first built works, but one of the key projects in his career, illustrating the spatial realization of the organic principle. The plan of the first scheme already contains the 'functional axis', leading from the entrance to the work room, which would serve to order the space in the final building. At this stage, the axis does not divide and/or link the kitchen and the living area. The kitchen is next to the living room in the northeast and the plan is still fully right-angled, with the rooms arranged in an L-shape. However the contours of the building form are dissolved in order to open up the plan. Each elevation is broken up with projections or recesses: the southwest façade is composed of five parts, marking externally the internal separations between rooms.

All of this made the project too expensive, so Scharoun developed a second scheme which tightened up the building mass, reducing both built area and volume. The plan retained only

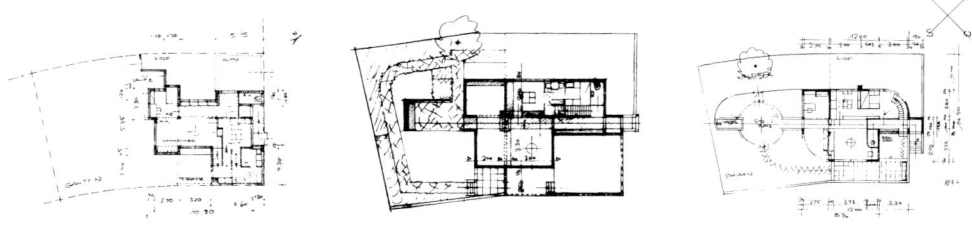

H. Scharoun, single-family house for the Werkbund exhibition 'Die Wohnung', Stuttgart-Weissenhof, 1927, development of plan.

the organization and tripartite division of the living area. The determining factor was now the 'functional axis', which ran from the entrance through the entire ground floor to the garden: here, the stairs became the effective means of distributing the space. The maid's quarters, basement stairs, kitchen and mezzanine were moved away from the west side and placed to the north of the 'functional axis'. This gave the west side the internal right angles that are so typical of the house. In contrast to the earlier scheme, the façades now appeared uninflected, with the exception of a projection on the southwest side. As there are no perspectives of this first scheme, we must assume that this plan was generated simply to explore the reduced spatial programme. Scharoun simplified the scheme: the axis now served to organize both circulation and space, and led from the entrance to the garden. The support spaces lay on one side of the axis, the living spaces on the other.

By now the basic concept was established. Had the house been built in this form, it would have corresponded better to the stated intentions of the organizers of the Weissenhof exhibition. It would have represented a significant step towards the realization of a typological model – and it would have been much cheaper. However it also had its weaknesses, which were clear in its external appearance. And when Scharoun re-worked the scheme, this was the aspect he concentrated on. The plan remained largely unaltered, but the exterior acquired marked cylindrical forms. To create a bigger garden, Scharoun pushed the house tight up against the northeast edge of the site. As a result, the entrance was dislodged from the axis. The stairs were moved to the north side: they no longer led directly to the first floor, but went in a curve that was reflected in the outer form of the façade. A second curve – at the southern corner of the living space – gave the plan a diagonal emphasis in addition to the strong central axis. Here we see for the first time a feature that became common in Scharoun's later designs – the use of diagonal spaces or lines of movement as a counterpart to parallel straight lines. The earlier scheme had also contained a secondary axis that subdivided the living area at the level of the workroom and introduced a change of level, marked by a few steps, between the small living room and the dining room. The third scheme contains the essential characteristics of the house as built, in particular the curve on the outside which followed the pitch of the stairs. By making the stairs visible, Scharoun created what Bodo Rasch called a 'trace form', and Hugo Häring a 'practical form'.

The final version of the house retained the spatial emphasis of a continuous line following the functional axis. The entrance was placed back on axis, the house was again set clear of the northeast boundary of the plot, and the garden wall was rounded off to emphasize the end of the building. An interesting formal change arose when the soffit, which had previously run the full length of the building, was reduced to cover only the terrace on the upper floor. For privacy and protection from the wind, Scharoun enlarged the northeast wall of the living room, turning it into a free-standing screening wall. He likewise extended the roof projection over the southeast terrace so that it functioned as a fixed awning and placed it at a 90-degree angle to the other screening wall. This gave the southeast side a distinct angularity in contrast to the rounded northwest side.

Scharoun's Weissenhof house was not unequivocally functional; nor did it fit neatly into either of Adolf Behne's dual categories of Modernism. As a consequence, critics paid it little attention, beyond commenting on its 'strange curved romanticism'. Though not in the mould of Cubist Modernism, the building was an extremely important step towards defining an 'intrinsic form'. The different stages of its development show that the principles of function and use were not the sole determinants of the plan and that many details were formally considered. Yet here for the first time the outer form corresponded to the living processes within.

The development of an organic method

From 1934 onwards, Scharoun defined the fundamental principles of his architecture, remaining open to different ideas and seeing every project as unique. At this time he began definitively to dissolve the right angle, the cube and the block in projects which are frequently described as marking his 'shift towards organic architecture', though they are clearly linked with earlier works such as the Weissenhof house. The difference is that their method of design was more influential and progressive.

The accepted wisdom is that Scharoun's organic design began with the Baensch House, which has a clearly formulated organic plan. However a comparison of Scharoun's most important plans from 1927 to 1939 shows a progressive move away from regular geometric forms. Although some projects still had a cubic external form, there was a step-by-step dissolution of the right angle and a free arrangement of volumes with round and/or obliquely cornered spaces. Forms began to evolve as the orthogonal grid was overlaid on the diagonal to give oblique angles and asymmetry. The Weissenhof plan still contains primary geometric forms. There are two circular segments at the ends of an implied diagonal which would generate oblique spaces if it were linked with the functional axis.

In the Schminke House, 1933, the diagonal becomes the ordering element, giving rise to unusual spatial compositions which Scharoun frequently returned to in later projects. Here we can see that the device of linking an orthogonal axis with a diagonal was not, as often maintained, a response to the particular conditions of a site, but rather a compromise between two methods of design: the organic-functional and the rather formally determined method of design.

A further development can be seen in the two schemes for a house for Professor Gocht, which links the living spaces in a different way. The wall is set at an angle, giving the hall a funnel shape, and the end wall of the living room is rounded off. The piano is turned slightly, so that it has a more direct relationship with the sitting area, while the room becomes basically organic.

From 1934 there was also a conscious change in the external 'style' of Scharoun's houses. The white render and ribbon windows gave way to brick and a more functional ordering. In the Mattern House the stone seems to unfold from the rendered wall, making it seem dissolved, unfinished.

Scharoun once remarked that the post-1937 houses had been designed 'under difficult circumstances'. While this was undoubtedly true, none of the contemporary documents indicates that the buildings were either refused planning permission or fundamentally altered by the planning authorities. The much-discussed 'shift from Functionalism' started early on: it was progressive, and was not triggered solely by the Nazis taking over the planning authorities. The plans and interiors of the houses were more innovative and unusual than those of the 1920s, but they were concealed behind relatively plain exteriors.

In his lectures at the Technische Universität in Berlin between 1946 and 1958, Scharoun referred explicitly to a project which illustrates well this change – the preliminary design for the Möller House, which drew on the ideas of Hugo Häring and Martin Heidegger. The two-storey house sits on a steep slope overlooking the Teetzen and Zermützel lakes. The elongated plan corresponds approximately to the profile of the nearby mountain top: the living space is orientated to give views over the lakes. The ground floor is arranged in three distinct parts, showing a clear separation between the rational, orthogonal support and sleeping areas and the more freely formed, oblique living area which had become almost a paradigm for Scharoun at the time. In the southeast of the house is the work area and garage. Next is the middle section, with a central staircase, hallway and living room. Joining the western corner of the living room is a trapezoidal sunken studio with a panoramic bow window. At the other end of the house, views to the east are opened up by the large bow window in the hallway next to the entrance. There are further views over the lakes from the living room.

H. Scharoun, house for Professor Gocht, project, 1934, and variant.

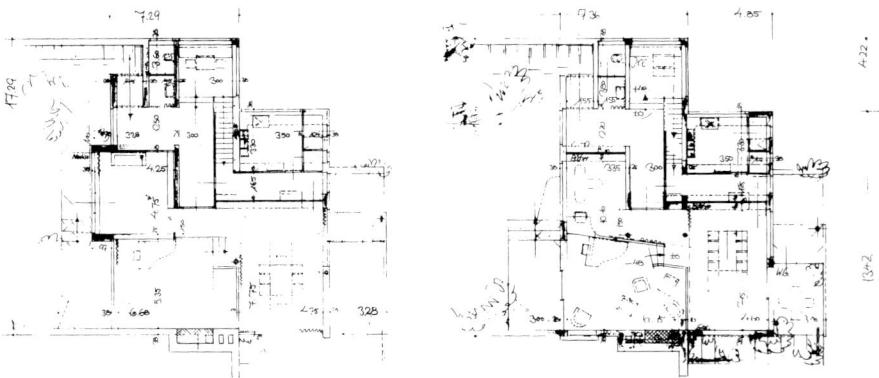

The preliminary design of the Möller House responds not only to the site and surrounding landscape, but also to the special needs of the client. The dynamic spatial sequence acts with the landscape and function to shape every aspect of the design.

It is hard to determine whether the change in Scharoun's work was triggered by socio-political circumstances, or by Hugo Häring, as Scharoun himself sometimes maintained. Historically, however, it is interesting to note that this change took place in the early 1930s, just as Modernism was going through a period of reappraisal and the protagonists of the International Style were leaving Germany. The influence of these external events should not be underestimated, for although the 'organic line' was evident in Scharoun's earlier work, his projects have a quite distinct character from the early 1930s on.

Hugo Häring is constantly referred to as the spiritual father of Scharoun, a role confirmed by Scharoun's frequent references to Häring and his theory of building in his lectures and talks after 1945. Scharoun also supported the publication of Häring's works and attempted to bring him out of 'exile' in Biberach to Berlin, so that he would have the opportunity to build again. In 1948 he wrote: 'The work of Hugo Häring was widely known before 1933, but has scarcely been talked about since. He has been hushed up, and his profound knowledge of our problems [of urban planning] shut off from us.'[11] When Scharoun spoke in his lectures of Häring's influence on his own work, he always referred to projects after 1934. However he also tried, in retrospect, to map out a historical evolution of organic building starting in 1918.[12] Häring's perspective, stated in 1946, was that: '– in Germany, Scharoun was already moving wholly in the realm of the organic, in space as multi-dimensional as a tree.'[13] Hugo Häring's writings should be taken into account, as Scharoun had not developed his own architectural theory by the Second World War.

Häring was concerned with the question of functional form and the architectonics of structural innovation at that time. As early as 1925, in his seminal essay 'wege zur form', he placed functional forms above expressive forms, since they '– already possess a form which

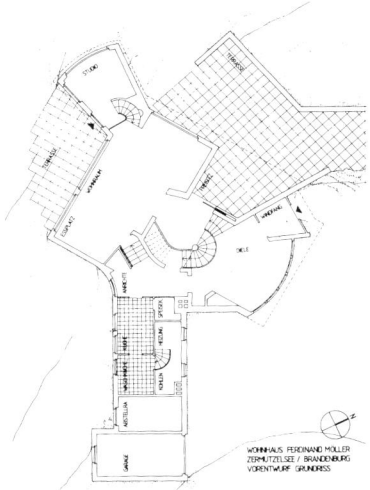

H. Scharoun, Ferdinand Möller house, Zermützelsee, near Altruppin, 1937, preliminary design, reconstruction.

fully satisfies our demands for a gesture –'[14] He wrote that in earlier cultures expression had determined form, but now there was a spiritual change which allowed a new way of generating more in line with the pure fulfilment of purpose: 'There is a method of generating form, in which all forms, both geometrical and crystalline, are individually conceived; the old method, on the other hand, requires the form of things to be determined from the outside, contrary to their own inherent form.'[15]

Häring was opposed to geometric preconceptions of any kind, even those derived from nature, like crystal. This meant he was also opposed to the utopian-crystalline architectural vision of the Crystal Chain circle centred around Bruno Taut. Not unexpectedly, Häring was never a member of this group. Crystalline glass peaks figure in the drawings of Scharoun before 1924, but not in those of Häring. Though Häring can be seen as a (temporary) 'link between Expressionism and the New Architecture',[16] he rejected the notion of expression as an end in itself. In contrast to Scharoun, he recognized that this was a weakness with the 'Glass Expressionists', even though they based their work on the forms of nature. Just as Adolf Behne had criticized Scharoun's imitation of nature, Häring emphasized that what was important was the process by which nature generated form, and not the repetition of organic or natural forms: 'We act in a similarly false way, if we take things back to basic geometric or crystalline forms, because we are again using force against them (Le Corbusier). The basic geometric forms are not original, ur-forms [but rather] derived abstractions, ordering principles.'[17]

The aesthetic which Häring referred to as 'organic beauty' arose almost of its own accord from the 'Essence of Things'. Häring's pronouncements on aesthetics and proportion were almost always negatively phrased: he described only how the New Building should *not* look and repeatedly quoted historic theories of proportion. In Le Corbusier Häring saw the latest, perhaps the last, representative of the Latin tradition of geometric laws of form and harmony: 'Le Corbusier is a classicist: he carries the line of the Greeks, the Romans and the Renaissance into our times. He stands apart from those Modernists who strive for an organic building.'[18]

In 1934 Häring once more outlined the split in Modernism that had become clear during the CIAM Congress in La Sarraz, Switzerland, in 1928. On that occasion, Le Corbusier had gained converts to his concept of Modern architecture and urban planning at the expense of Häring's view of an organic New Architecture. From that time, Häring was seen as the opponent of Le Corbusier, but the real confrontation – which concerned the fundamental principles of Modern architecture – was between the German Ring Group and the CIAM group around Sigfried Giedion and Le Corbusier. Häring sought to justify his theory on historic grounds. He maintained that he belonged to a time whose cultural will was 'undoubtedly an organic structure'.

For Häring, the historical progression of cultures clearly led towards an organic culture and/or conception of art and architecture. A major portion of his writings is taken up with developing this theory and laying the foundations for an organic New Architecture. Häring referred to an 'autonomy of form' and assigned individually differentiated architectural forms to specific cultures. According to him, each primary form was 'an independent entity governed by its own internal laws –'.[19] Different cultures had adopted different geometric forms: the Egyptians built with the pyramid, the Greeks with the rectangle, the Romans with the arch, circle and dome. He established a correlation between the formal expression of a culture and its political system. Thus, for example, the political system of the Greeks corresponded to the 'Essence' of the rectangle: 'hard-edged democracy – without any expansive tendencies, remaining assuredly within the bounds of its contours, and going no further, it gives rise to the city-state and the citizen. No element of the rectangle permits the formation of compartments or layers, no element permits individuals to amass or maintain power – So the rectangle acts as an essential principle contributing to the fate of an individual culture and of the Greeks.'[20]

According to this theory, architecture reflects the governing principle behind the socio-political structure of a culture. Thus the development of the arch, circle and dome was tied to the rise of the new determining power of Rome. Häring contrasted this universal 'geometric principle' with the 'organic creation of form', which began from the inside and worked outwards, and he proposed that only a humane, democratic, mass-orientated society could produce a culture with an organic creative form. Historically, the Gothic style was seen to have been determined by individuals, and not by geometric forms. The Gothic was therefore, according to Häring, an example of the transition from the geometric principle to the organic principle. Häring had a teleological conception of history. He wrote: 'Cultures evolve in accordance with a natural law, with a definite goal in sight.'[21] Individuals carried out this natural law, but had no control over the direction it took. In all cases, the goal was an 'organic culture': the Gothic – the expression of Northern Europe and the essence of the Germanic people – was a step towards this goal.

The planning of Berlin

Immediately after the war Scharoun found the opportunity to evolve a comprehensive theory of architecture with his appointment to several official and public posts. He was a city councillor and Head of the Greater Berlin Department of Building and Housing from 1945 to 1946; Professor in the faculty of architecture at the Technische Universität in Berlin from 1946 to 1958; and Head of the Institute for Building Science at the German Academy of Sciences in Berlin from 1947 to 1950.

Scharoun's concern was to consolidate the premises of organic architecture that Häring had formulated in his writings from 1924 onwards. But whereas Häring directed his work at a small, theoretically orientated audience, Scharoun attempted, in the years after the war, to expand the basis of organic architecture and bring it into the public consciousness. The time seemed right: people's attitudes and practices were changing, and there was a greater receptiveness to other 'organic models' such as the architecture of Frank Lloyd Wright and the 'organic urban planning' of Hans Bernhard Reichow.[22] At first it seemed as if Scharoun would be able to translate the theories that had 'developed in obscurity' into large-scale architectural and urban-planning projects. But this failed to happen. Instead, post-war architecture entered the period of reconstruction which we know, with hindsight, to have been characterized by mistakes and bad planning. Scharoun's own career suffered. Total planning remained largely a utopian concept, and organic models were discarded around the time of the currency reform, just a few years after the war. In the ensuing period of 'restoration', many key positions were given back to the people who had held them during the war. From today's perspective, the short-lived phase of progressive, idealistic planning appears like a period of make-believe. By the time the rubble was being cleared to make way for reconstruction, the practitioners had regained their hold.

After Scharoun lost his job as city planner in 1947, Häring wrote, symbolically, that a man 'who would have built pyramids for the Pharaohs' had been sent into the wilderness because his planning was alleged to be uneconomical.[23] The changing mood was also evident during the debate at the Darmstadt symposium in 1951. There, the older generation, represented by Scharoun, Paul Bonatz and Otto Bartning, maintained the old positions and counter-positions, while the younger generation were interested in nothing but their pragmatic mega-plans for the future.

Returning, however, to the immediate post-war period, Scharoun was appointed Head of the Greater Berlin Department of Housing and Building on 17 May 1945, shortly after the surrender of the German forces. Scharoun later described this turn of events as 'surprising',[24] but it was not really so, for he had been brought out of 'exile' by Gropius, who had secured his appointment through the American military authorities.[25] One major factor in his favour was that both the American and the British military authorities insisted that important jobs should go only to architects who had not been involved with any of the Third Reich's large planning schemes – and such architects were thin on the ground. In addition, the Modernists were attempting to re-establish old contacts to take advantage of what appeared to be a growing 'sense of attonement'. Accordingly, Gropius also gave Scharoun the task of setting up a new German CIAM group.

Scharoun formed a collective which produced a plan for the reconstruction of Greater Berlin, unsanctioned by the Allies.[26] The group's main intention was to counter the general feeling of uncertainty with a plan conceived from the German standpoint, to make a political gesture by saying that there had to be a clear principle behind the planning of Greater Berlin: that it was not enough to just clear away the rubble. The planning group within the collective included a number of architects who had been active participants in the pre-war CIAM Congresses, most notably Wils Ebert and Selman Selmanagic.[27] Scharoun later stated that the intention of the collective had been to create an 'urban landscape' that reflected the spirit and structure of the medieval city, but not its appearance.[28]

The collective believed that the historical concentric development of Berlin had impeded effective traffic planning and land use, and therefore proposed an alternative – a series of parallel 'residential and commercial areas, each developed around its own core'.[29] The residential areas were to be concentrated in well-defined 'neighbourhoods', small enough to be crossed on foot in ten to fifteen minutes. These neighbourhoods would contain school buildings, cultural facilities and, where possible, places of work, to minimize the need for road travel. Major road axes both linked the different neighbourhoods and acted as boundaries between them: to avoid traffic congestion, the roads ran parallel to each other, and not towards a common centre. The layout of the road network and residential areas followed the east-west axis of the Spree valley. Where possible the plan made use of existing streets, but extended them to form an orthogonal traffic grid.

The 'collective plan' was presented to the public in 1946 in an exhibition, 'Berlin plans – a first report', in the white hall of the (then still intact) Berlin Castle.[30] The plan was admittedly utopian and primarily intended to provoke further discussion – in fact, it unleashed wide-

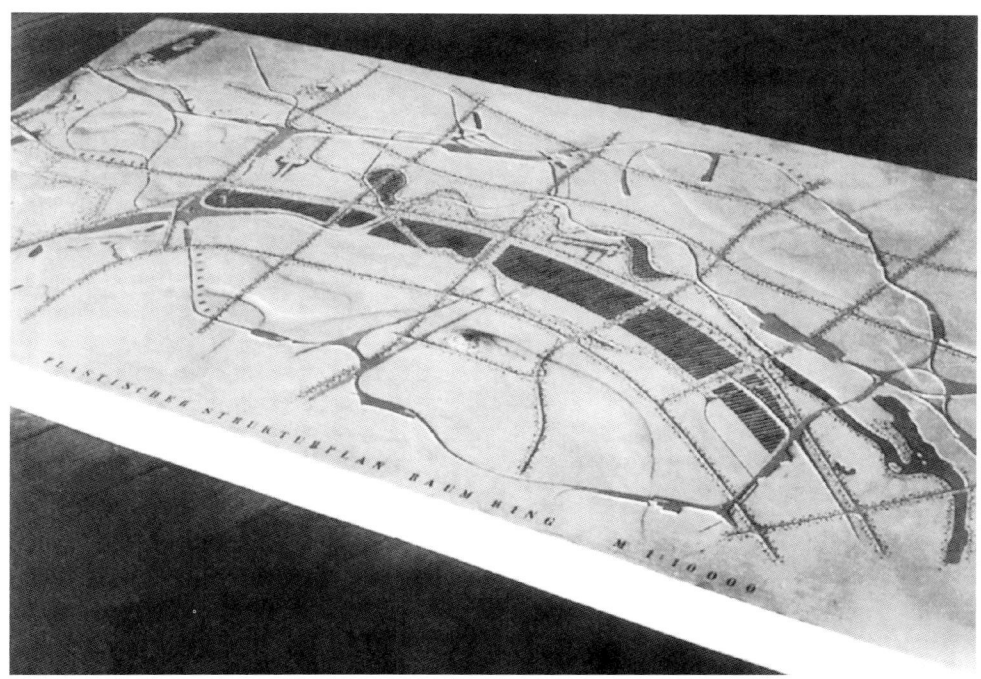
Berlin plans – a first report, plan for the reconstruction of Berlin, 1946, the so-called 'collective plan'.

spread criticism, on account of its schematic division of residential and working areas, supply networks and traffic systems. The most common complaint was that the plan did not show due respect for the historical structure of the city, though it was of course a deliberate, radical departure from the axial planning of Martin Mächler and Albert Speer. Critics also noted the plan's failure to address immediate problems such as clearing the rubble and providing housing. The most negative responses came from the very planners who would later embark on their own wholesale 'cleaning up' of the city.

Some of the criticism of the plan was aimed at Scharoun in person, and the revival of German Modernism that he represented – as the headline in the *Wirtschaftszeitung* of 6 December 1946 made clear: 'Berlin plans – Werkbund and Bauhaus traditions prevail on the fields of ruin'. And in 1947, following Scharoun's dismissal from his post in the city's Department of Housing and Building, Rudolf Pfister wrote in *Baumeister*: 'Perhaps Prof. Scharoun would make a notable poet, but it is hard to imagine him as a teacher of the young. His obvious predilection for solutions that appear ingenious, regardless of cost, is all too painfully reminiscent of the ideology of certain doctrinarian art historians close to the Bauhaus circle.'[31]

On issues of urbanism, the collective plan was contradictory, a reflection of the different positions of its members. It addressed the issue of future growth with provisions for decentralization, a development of the urban landscape, and a linking of commercial and residential districts in the inner city. However the zoning of urban functions and the network of limited-access urban motorways were clearly derived from the principles of the Athens Charter. Today, the collective plan is still blamed for the hybrid planning of the autonomous City of Berlin, although the main damage was caused by Modernist models.

Consolidating an organic architecture

The failure of the collective plan had far-reaching consequences for Scharoun. In the years that followed he had more opportunity to concentrate on his design work and put forward his concept of organic building. He entered practically all the major competitions for schools, theatres and concert halls, but did not get any commissions until the Kassel Theatre in 1953. The Romeo and Juliet pair of high-rises, 1954–1959, was in fact his first built project after the war. Between 1947 and 1952, Scharoun developed his basic principles, both theoretical and practical, of organic building. Between 1947 and 1950 he was appointed Head of the Institute for Building Science in Berlin. There, he hoped to establish an atmosphere of pure research which would provide the guidelines for a future architecture of reconstruction.[32] His prime concern was the 'intensification of the organic principle' and its basic tenets. But Scharoun's ideas were not taken up: Häring's fear that he was not suited to such an academic environment proved well founded, and he left the Institute in 1950.

During this period Scharoun also worked on a number of projects that represent important developments of his ideas, though they were never built: the housing in Friedrichshain (1949); the Darmstadt elementary school (1951), which had a clear influence on later schools in Marl and Lünen; and the Kassel Theatre (1952), which seemed to mark a turning point.

Up until the mid 1960s Scharoun wrote numerous texts which set out a theoretical framework for his organic building methods. In these writings, he made frequent reference to Häring and adopted his most important theories and lines of argument. Accordingly, he proposed that the history of mankind was a genetic process over which individuals had little control. At first architecture had been governed by geometry, but the Gothic period had ignited a period of change which was leading inexorably to organic building. If the organic was not already in place, it was because this genetic process was either being ignored or actively restricted by the people in power.

Like Häring, Scharoun believed that only organic building was capable of expressing the spiritual and functional Essence of a culture or a building type. The issue was to find form, rather than have one imposed by the rigid principle of geometry. In order to achieve this, it was necessary to recognize and accept that the design would be determined by a single predominant philosophy or concept of culture. At this time, in the 1950s, society seemed unable to change fast enough to keep up with advances in technology, science and industrial production. Even the optimism of the years of reconstruction could not provide an ideal framework in the long term. Scharoun noted that without the support of a universal idea, people tended to lose their identity and orientate themselves towards the past. In 1957 he gave what could be seen as an early warning about the historicist regressions of Post-Modernism: 'People look for something to sustain them in face of the turbulent events of everyday existence. If they do not find this support, they flee out of their own time into an alien time. They latch onto the styles of the past and try them all out in turn.'[33]

Scharoun differentiated between the practical form and the organic form: '– the practical form derives from function, whereas the organic form is determined by the range of physiological and psychological relationships between the subject and the object.'[34] For Scharoun, the practical form was exemplified by Eric Lyons's housing development in Richmond, the organic form by Häring's single-family homes in Biberach. Here we see a decisive difference between Scharoun's interpretation of the organic and that of this mentor. Häring saw function as the starting-point for all building: the role of the organic, in his view, was to generate form. Scharoun, on the other hand, granted the organic form an autonomy, leaving room for irrational elements which did not strictly correspond to the fulfilment of function.

For Häring the relationship between geometry and the organic paralleled the relationship between the masses and the individual. He believed that the fulfilment of function, combined with the organic method of generating form, would 'individualize' the building – in contrast to the primary geometry applied to specific building tasks by architects such as Schinkel in the past. For Häring, these typological forms represented a widely recognizable demand for power by the masses – and a rejection of the power of the individual within the community.[35] Scharoun applied the same principle to the situation of his own time, saying that the tension between the northern and the Mediterranean countries was an indication of the 'position of the individual *vis-à-vis* the community or the masses, seen in the light of the static or the dynamic'.[36]

Scharoun stated unequivocally that organic architecture grew out of, and perpetuated, the relationship of the individual to the surrounding community. He believed that by creating common spaces and facilities for social activities, by giving form to the 'middle ground' of social interaction, he could foster an awareness of the community which would counteract de-individualization, collectivization and the power of propaganda. 'The seeds of an organically formed community lie at grassroots level, in these sorts of facilities – Unless we acknowledge this and take care, the end result will always be a society organized from above such as we experienced, with all its destructive consequences, under Hitler.'[37]

For Häring and Scharoun the New Architecture was also a political declaration. The organic principle of generating form corresponded to the democratic principle of free will. Immediately after the war Häring stated clearly that the New Architecture had to be made more democratic: 'My dear Ministers of Culture! Where are your eyes? Are they in the museum, too? Does it mean nothing to you that the Old Architecture knowingly colluded with Hitler's aims?'[38] In this matter, also, Scharoun adopted Häring's ideas, saying that each building should be based on the 'universal principle of democracy': 'The New Architecture strives – in a broad sense – for a natural, organic order.'[39] For this, the essential precondition was not a uniform artistic will, but rather an agreed ethical position. In architecture, philosophical and moral considerations had to play a decisive role in determining the design, and not be stifled by economic pressures – as Scharoun so often found in the years of the German 'economic miracle'.

Häring's and Scharoun's views reflected the general mood in Germany right after the war. Memories of the conflict were still vivid, and it was seen as important for architecture to achieve a democratic expression. But although this principle was enshrined in many of the official building guidelines of the time, it had limited practical effect, because architects like Häring and Scharoun were unable to provide workable instructions on design or form. By their own standards, they excluded themselves.

Building for the community
Along with social housing, cultural facilities were a major theme of Scharoun's work after the Second World War. These projects again illustrate the concerns that ran like a *leitmotif* through his life, from the period of Expressionism onwards. In 1949 Scharoun drew up the first designs for an opera house in Leipzig and a recital hall in Stuttgart. In 1952 he won the Kassel Theatre competition, which should have given him the opportunity to complete his first major building. In the event, this opportunity did not come until 1956, when he started work on the Berlin Philharmonie, the commission which won him belated fame and secured further work from 1963 on.

It was in the area of theatre design, however, that Scharoun made his most significant contribution to contemporary architecture, in terms of both theory and design. From the beginning, Scharoun saw the form and content of theatre as an important reflection of the culture of a society. In 1920, as a 27-year-old, he wrote of his watercolour schemes for a theatre within a cultural centre at Gelsenkirchen: 'Far away from the constricting structures of conventional theatre space, the people sit between walls that have been decorated with them in mind and the action unfolds around the stage, ruling out alienation. The space and the action are boldly brought to the people. Form, common consciousness and common experience, in buildings, things and people, are a recurrent aspiration of our times – of Art and Life.'[40] Here already were the principal themes of Scharoun's theatre designs: the breaking up of the traditional theatre space, the linking of the stage and auditorium, and the attempt to find a new form of theatre capable of expressing the commonality and culture of society. More than 30 years after this, in 1952, Scharoun wrote of his project for Kassel: 'It is necessary to be aware of the meaning of the expressive forms, if the city as a whole is to be founded on a solid base of operative factors which can interact effectively with each other. From this viewpoint, it is clear why the new bourgeois society has made the "theatre" the vehicle for these factors which bear influence on the structure of society. The theatre combines universal issues with specific, often local interpretations and active responses, which are subject to constant change.'[41]

Scharoun's 1920 project for Gelsenkirchen already showed the building mass as a unified form, with the auditorium and stage combined to create a single space. The design, with its wide stage and semicircular auditorium, was similar in form to Poelzig's Salzburg Festspielhaus of 1920–1921, which was much discussed at the time. It also reflected Max Reinhardt's call for an integrated auditorium. In this early design, Scharoun retained the framework of the conventional proscenium stage, but broadened it and reduced the curve that usually gave rise to an unbalanced axial emphasis.

Scharoun's projects of the 1950s clearly continue the pre-war spirit of experimentation which attempted to take the theatre beyond its traditional 19th-century form. Streit's Reform Theatre in Vienna (1887), Van de Velde's Theatre for the 1914 Werkbund exhibition in Cologne, the projects of Poelzig, and Piscator's and Gropius's Total Theatre (1927) were all important developments which gave rise to a form of stage with an apron that projected far into the auditorium; a U-shaped auditorium; Weininger's Constructivist Theatre in the round; and finally, the Total Theatre, which united all possibilities within itself. The common factors in all these designs were the determination of space through a scenographic sequence and the attempt to combine the stage and auditorium to create a unified space.

Scharoun dealt most intensively with the issue of theatre design in the period of reconstruction following the Second World War. More than 40 new theatres were built in the boom years from 1950 to 1965. In rapid succession Scharoun worked on projects for the State Theatre in Kassel (1952), the National Theatre in Mannheim (1953) and the Gelsenkirchen Theatre (1954). But none of these was realized, and it was another ten years before Scharoun again tackled theatre design, with the 1964 Zürich competition. One year later, in 1965, he was able to start on his only built theatre: the Wolfsburg Municipal Theatre. Through all these projects, Scharoun developed a comprehensive theoretical approach to theatre design which made a significant contribution to the contemporary debate.

After the Second World War, most people working within the theatre favoured the multi-purpose hall — exemplified, in an elegant manner, by Mies van der Rohe's work in Mannheim. This was an extension of the total theatre concept of a variable space which could be adapted to the specific needs of each performance. But Scharoun was opposed to the notion of the multi-purpose hall because he thought that the different theatrical traditions of each city necessitated different theatre spaces. For him, the only solution in keeping with the times was the Space Theatre, which allowed the stage to be extended for greater flexibility but maintained a clear contrast between stage and auditorium.

Scharoun believed that this broad type of stage was flexible enough for all kinds of productions, even those conceived for the proscenium stage, because it related more directly to a single, undivided auditorium, drawing the audience into the action. One of the conventions that he wished to retain was the traditional symbolic content of the theatre: 'On both sides,' he wrote in 1953, ' the auditorium and the stage, the real and the unreal — the relationship of freedom to obligation should have the same importance. This pattern is reflected once more in the manner in which the stage and auditorium are defined at the rear. Here too the border — the boundary — has not only a technical but an Essential meaning.'[42]

For Scharoun the concept of 'intimacy' was crucial to the design of the space. A maximum auditorium capacity of 900 allowed spectators to participate fully in the on-stage action and dialogue. Scharoun also favoured the intimate theatre because it broke down established social hierarchies. The integrated auditorium contained no prestigious galleries or boxes. Instead there were open rows of seats, which made the best use of restricted space. In the broader social context, the theatre acted as the ultimate expression of the culture of a city. The importance of intimacy within the design process was emphasized by Scharoun in a lecture on 15 December 1952.[43] Another important factor was the notion of phenomenological 'Place', as defined by Heidegger. Each building had not only to respond to the recognizable forces that made up the immediate context in which it was set, but had also to take up the wider urban context formed by the traditions of a city, its traffic patterns, squares and spatial subdivisions. This planning process had a direct effect on the form of the building, guiding '– the way in which the line of action, the organic, evolves out of the Essential, taking into consideration the requirements of the time'.[44]

In Scharoun's view, one of the requirements of the time was for people to appropriate architecture, to 'get out and experience' the spaces, as he put it. In Wolfsburg the approach to the theatre is precisely defined, and a café and terrace on top of the foyer allow people to 'move around' the architecture. The blending of the building into the landscape, the unity of the man-made and the natural, further reinforces a sense of accessibility, in contrast to 19th-century theatres, which distanced themselves from the public through their imposing forms. Similarly the Kassel Theatre, examined below, is opened up by means of lines of circulation and a descent from the terrace over the rear stage to the Aue Park: 'Opening up buildings seems to me an extremely important means of drawing them into the realm of the community – over and above any apparent visual means.'[45]

The projects for the State Theatre in Kassel, the National Theatre in Mannheim and the a-perspective as a design principle

The Kassel Theatre competition in 1953 presented Scharoun with his first opportunity to apply the principles of organic architecture to a large project. The brief was to replace a 19th-century theatre that had been destroyed during the Second World War. In his detailed explanatory text, Scharoun outlined the historical development of the site in the city's Friedrichplatz and concluded that instead of closing off the square, as the old theatre had done, the new building should establish an obvious relationship to the Aue Park behind it. In this way the building form would respond to the historical conditions of its context, rather that restore the 19th-century planning, which he saw as misguided.

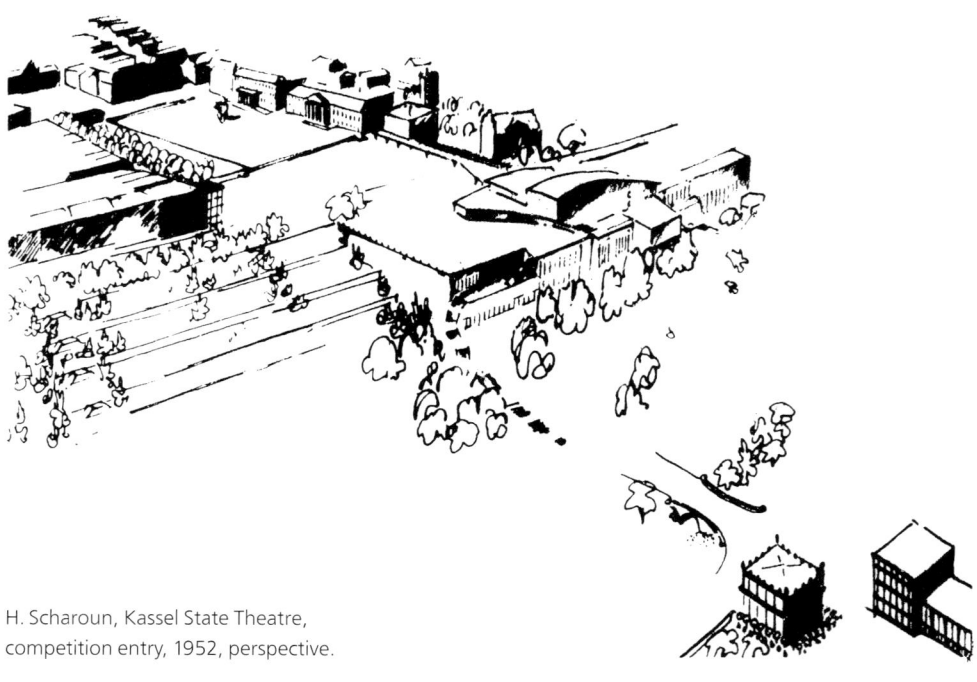

H. Scharoun, Kassel State Theatre, competition entry, 1952, perspective.

Correspondingly, Scharoun's theatre complex is set slightly off the axis of the Friedrichplatz, in order to open up views of the landscape. A sense of closure is achieved with a fly-tower whose asymmetrical curving form embraces the spaces in front, rather than towering above them. The front parts of the building – the auditorium, foyer and entrance area – are not tied together formally, but are arranged as a series of distinct spaces which terrace down to the square. The fly-tower skilfully links the side stages, technical and ancillary spaces. To the right of the main stage, within the remaining walls of the original theatre, there is a studio theatre linked to the scene stores via the side stage of the main theatre.

The shape of the main theatre was determined by the broad open stage which Scharoun developed in collaboration with the set designer Willem Huller. The stage surround had a low horizon, in order to 'make use of the latest developments in lighting technology'. In front of the auditorium was a series of differentiated spaces – foyer, cloakrooms, a garden courtyard and a snack bar – which opened like windbreaks, setting curved elements against each other. Visitors to the theatre would have experienced a series of constantly changing and colliding spaces – a sensation Scharoun later recreated in the foyers of the Philharmonie and the Wolfsburg Theatre. Though the space appears irrational, it is in fact clearly ordered. The visitor enters the foyer and ticket office either from the main approach or from the pedestrian bridge above. To the right are cloakrooms for that side of the auditorium; beyond the cloakrooms are stairs which lead down to the stalls and up to the circle. A further passage from the foyer leads directly to the stalls and the lobby on the right-hand side of the lower level. The vertical organization is thus also broken up by a complex horizontal arrangement.

The Kassel Theatre competition was one of the most shameful episodes of German post-war architecture, an example of the misdirection that has contributed to the state of current architecture. The jury met from 17–19 September 1952 and, after examining 116 entries, awarded first prize to Scharoun. The jury comprised, amongst others, the architects Hebebrand, Bartning, Eiermann and Kallmorgen, all of whom made a considerable contribution to this decision. Scharoun's progressive design initially was judged very positively. The jury noted, emphatically, that the project expressed a new sense of hope for the future, proposing a fundamental new architecture to accompany the new state. (In art, this sense of hope found expression in the setting up of Documenta 1955 in Kassel.) The jury also praised the integration of the scheme with the broader urban context.[46] Indeed, for years, the plans and model of the theatre were to make an impact in successive exhibitions around the country.

However no sooner had the prize been awarded than the authorities began openly to question the buildability of the project. Preliminary works dragged on as Scharoun revised the design. The foundation stone was finally laid on 15 October 1954, but the building authorities had not provided Scharoun with any plans of the old foundations, and after a short time workers ran into the remains of demolished fortifications and filled-in undercrofts. Instead of undertaking deeper excavations for the foundations, the authorities immediately halted construction, and on 2 June 1955 dismissed Scharoun's design team. They already had another man for the job, having commissioned Paul Bode on 2 February 1955 to 'examine the possibilities for building a theatre on the given site'. Bode, who had played no part in the competition, was able to deliver 1:50 working drawings for the theatre just a few weeks after the cancellation of Scharoun's project – by which point, we may conclude, he had been working on the design for at least a year.

Scharoun's entry to the Mannheim competition of 1953 proposes an a-perspectival theatre space, in which the stage and auditorium are both skewed and divided up by a low S-shaped ramp. Scharoun wrote a comprehensive text on the a-perspectival space entitled 'On the Structure of the Theatre Building'.[47] There, he described two different directions in the historical development of the theatre: the axial theatre of Italy and France, which was tied to the notion of the perspective, in contrast to the enclosed space of the Greeks, the itinerant theatre of the Christian Mystery plays, and the theatre of Shakespeare, which all corresponded to the a-perspective theatre space.

The form of the a-perspectival theatre responds to two dimensions of man's existence: the earthly-physical dimension and the meta-physical dimension, which transcends physical nature. Drama based on this conception has an irrational character. Conversely, the perspective theatre, represented primarily by classical French tragedy and comedy, has a rational basis. Its conflicts mainly arise from the differing aims and intentions of different characters. The rational theatre was conceived for the deep perspective stages and axial auditoriums of Renaissance and Baroque theatres. The perspective is tied to the physiological composition of the eye and the rational categories of space and time. It can only present objects as physical entities – an experience far removed from the recognition of phenomenological 'Essence'.

Scharoun saw the dichotomy between the rational and the irrational theatre, or French and Shakespearean drama, as the historical foundation of contemporary theatre. In the case of Germany, the elemental power of Shakespeare proved decisive, inspiring the 18th-century writers who were searching for their own voice. Shakespeare provided the characters of the 'fool' and the 'robber', and the foundations for 'Faust'. The world of 'Faust', like that of the Christian Mystery play and Shakespeare, is a-perspectival. Faust is led – by his own autonomous feelings and thoughts – into a chain of events from which he cannot escape until death comes to release his metaphysical being. Faust is irrational theatre.

In Scharoun's view, the divide between spirit and space became increasingly pronounced around the turn of the century. Max Reinhardt attempted to give a spiritual dimension to his stage sets by subjugating them to the dialogue. But it was ultimately Expressionism which pierced the outer shell of the senses and tried to make visible what could not be seen. The set was made to suggest both in words and in unspoken drama a hidden area of conflict. For Scharoun this was the inheritance of the modern theatre. The tradition of the north, in his eyes, was clearly the irrational theatre.

In Mannheim, the selection of the site was determined by its sociological significance. The theatre's siting, surroundings and relationship to the city all had spiritual relevance. Scharoun did not place the theatre within Mannheim's orthogonal plan, because that would have made it subordinate to the built space around it. Instead, he set the building in an open space, its 'Place'; distinguished by a cosmic quality and a universal power of reference. However, according to Scharoun, a true link between the people and the stage could not be expressed by the exterior alone: the new form of theatre required also a new interior. The axial interior of the rational theatre treats the public as a homogeneous mass of individual subjects. The irrational theatre, on the other hand, is a place of commonality, of dialogue between heaven and earth. This points to an important element: the educational function of the irrational theatre. Greek drama called upon the individual to act responsibly and to contribute to the development of the political society: it drew the attention of the people away from the Dionysian circle towards the Apollonian rectangle.

The irrational theatre appealed to the spiritual nature of the audience. It took them from the perspective into an 'a-perspectival' realm, from a space of mass and frontality into a space of emotion and movement, in which they became a community. The 'Place' of such a community was defined not by a specific architecture, but rather by a spatial ordering, which allowed room for inner emotions. Following the a-perspective principle the auditorium is ordered into different sectors which offer varied views of the action on the stage. The role of the spectator was to react. This was the organic solution to the question of communication between the stage and the people.

The concept of the 'a-perspective' was adopted by Scharoun from the Swiss cultural philosopher Jean Gebser who wrote about the foundations and manifestations of an a-perspectival world.[48] Gebser divided the representational arts into three consecutive periods. The first period, which he called 'unperspectival', lasted until the Renaissance; it was followed by the 'perspectival' period, which was being replaced in present times by the 'a-perspectival' period.[49] Gebser drew a parallel between the emergence of perspective in art and the history of spiritual development. Gebser's divisions of time corresponded to Häring's theory of a teleological natural law, with its progression from geometric to organic culture.[50] What Gebser called perspectival and a-perspectival, Häring called geometric and organic. According to Gebser, the transition to the a-perspective had been triggered by the new representational forms of the Cubists, who in their sculpture and painting extended the two-dimensionality of surfaces and the three-dimensionality of perspective representation into a fourth dimension – time. Scharoun had already referred to the representation of time in the description of his Darmstadt project. Similarly, the Mannheim Theatre, in contrast to the traditional theatre, 'expressed in the ordering of movement and in the sequence of events the focusing properties of "places", the juxtaposition and superposition of time within a whole – on the basis of the physical representation of time.'[51] To express the element of time within space, it was necessary to dispense with the rigid framework which permitted only a consecutive sequence of action through time. To allow simultaneous action and changing scenes, Scharoun opened up the stage, giving it the function of 'differentiating and ordering'. 'The audience is placed in the most vivid relationship to the stage – the audience is activated: it accompanies, follows the change of place, which is itself determined by a primary principle. The rigid axis is thus overcome.'[52] Expressing the same notion, Gebser wrote: 'The new architecture builds in order to express this physically, no more rigidly defined rooms, but a space-time continuum. In other words: time, in so far as it can be represented architecturally, has transformed the closed three-dimensional architectural space into a moving, open space-time.'[53]

Gebser believed that the a-perspectival element was being expressed through the spectrum of modern architecture. Unlike Häring, he did not differentiate between the organic and the geometry of Le Corbusier. But Scharoun's a-perspectival theatre design for Mannheim went beyond the historic rules, appropriating Gebser's theory and attempting physically to represent the fourth dimension of time in space.

Ludwig Mies van der Rohe, Mannheim National Theatre, competition entry, 1953.

The Mannheim National Theatre competition of 1953 was one of the most interesting of the post-war period. It attracted a wide range of entries and showed clearly the contrasting styles of Mies van der Rohe and Scharoun (later made manifest in the Kulturforum in Berlin). The terms of the competition allowed the architects great freedom: even the choice of site was left open. Scharoun set his project in the Goetheplatz, which was the site of the final building. The old town of Mannheim had an orthogonal grid-iron of streets running mainly north, south, east and west. Scharoun attempted to subvert this grid with the mass of the building without altering the rectangular Goetheplatz. His idea, which was simple but effective, was to place the building diagonally in the square, in line with the similarly oblique main street. The main building mass, which brought together the stage and administrative area, stands on a diagonal. The masses of the small and large auditoriums, positioned at each corner, stand at an angle to the rest of the building. The outer form of the building also indicates the main theme of the interior: asymmetry. To express the a-perspective element, the opening of the stage is 27 metres wide; the main stage, therefore, is of shallower proportions in order to emphasize the progression of the scenes. The stalls are divided into three sections and set slightly off axis, at an angle to the stage.

To accompany the change of place in the staging of scenes, there was a new system of lighting. The wide stage opening could be divided with a 'light curtain' into different sectors, so that individual scenes in the dramatic action could be 'softly faded out'. The stage itself was divided into three skewed zones that corresponded to defined areas of action. Under the roof of the auditorium were floodlights in 'gondola-shaped housings' which could be moved horizontally and vertically to follow the action. These moving lights were shown quite vividly in Scharoun's colour sketches of the project. Daylight could be brought into both theatres: in the main theatre, it could even be controlled by a mechanically operated flap in the roof.

In his project description, Scharoun referred repeatedly to the multi-functional nature of the stage – a major requirement for theatres at the time. He even emphasized that the stage could also be used for the perspective theatre. Häring considered this unfeasible – such plays were in conflict with the whole concept of the design – and he told Scharoun in a letter not to 'covet box office success' and instead to focus on the fact that he had created a stage for the future.[54]

But ultimately the Mannheim Theatre, like the one in Kassel before it, was built by an architect who had not even taken part in the competition. First, ten practices were invited to take part in a limited competition: Mies van der Rohe, Scharoun, Schwarz/Riphahn/Bernhard, Döcker, Schweizer, Perrottet/Stoecklin/Baur, Lange/Mitzlaff, Schmechel/Thoma, Marx/Wagner/Au and Plattner/Mündel. Mies was placed second, Scharoun third. In September 1953 Mies, Schwarz/Riphahn and Schweizer were invited to develop their designs, but in addition Gerhard Weber was commissioned to produce a scheme. And Weber's scheme – a patent copy of Mies's theatre, with its clear, cubic form and combination of both stages and vertical fly-tower – was duly built.

The Zürich Schauspielhaus project and the Wolfsburg Municipal Theatre

Following the failure of his third theatre design of the 1950s, in Gelsenkirchen, Scharoun did not participate in any more theatre competitions until 1964, when he produced a design for the Zürich Schauspielhaus. The project shows a closed building mass, similar in principle to the Berlin Philharmonie. But whereas the Philharmonie is defined by curving lines and strongly pitched roofs, the Zürich building has a crystalline character, with more emphasis on

H. Scharoun, Zürich Schauspielhaus, competition entry, 1952, model from east.

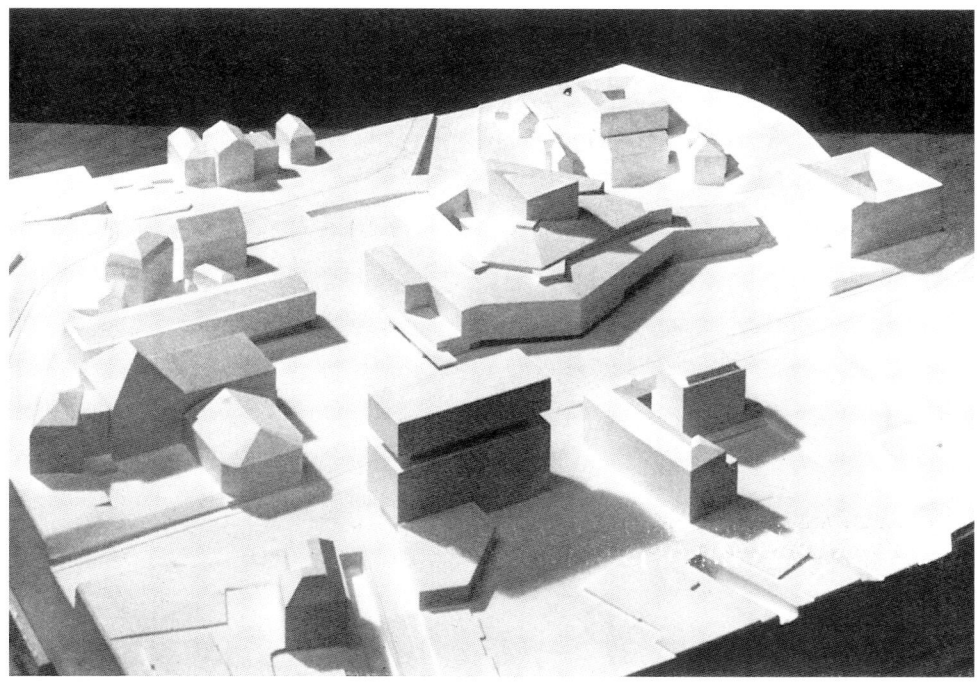

formal and representational elements. In contrast to earlier designs, in which the stage and administrative areas were brought together in a formal dialogue, the Zürich project had a five-cornered fly-tower which rose up from the centre of the building to provide an aesthetic focal point, similar to many other theatres of the time. The competition for Zürich specified a traditional proscenium stage: in the brief Max Frisch argued that it was necessary to return to the traditional separation between stage and audience because there were no plays for the new stage forms.[55] Frisch's status as an architect and playwright ensured that this text had a far-reaching impact. By 1964 most of the post-war German theatres had been built and the experiments in new forms of stage and auditorium were over.

In the Zürich project Scharoun managed, within the confines of a fully symmetrical auditorium and proscenium stage, to bring the audience into an a-perspectival relationship with the action on the stage. This was achieved by means of a 'tilted stage' with a ramp that projected at a sharp angle into the auditorium. By doubling the shallow a-perspective stage used at Mannheim and linking it to a projecting apron and proscenium, he created a five-cornered stage form. However this design was unsuccessful: the first prize went to Jörn Utzon's proposal for a simple proscenium stage, which was not built.

In Wolfsburg, Scharoun was finally given the opportunity to build a theatre, although he did not live to see its completion in 1973. The town was the headquarters of Volkswagen, with a similar lustre on the cultural map, someone once said, to Manaos, in Brazil, 'which once had a visit from Caruso'.[56] Scharoun managed none the less to overcome cuts in the programme and build a convincing theatre which was the final scene in his public architecture, following the climax of the Philharmonie.

The main elevation extends from the foyer in the southeast to the administrative area in the northwest, placing the theatre in full view of the city. Viewed from the east, the theatre aligns itself with the hill which rises away from the city hall. From the south, it consists of a loose sequence of buildings distributed around the slope of the hill, forming a focal point for the inner city, a 'city crown'. The theatre is framed against the backdrop of the wooded hilltop; in the foreground it has a gentle green slope.

In addition to the theatre design, Scharoun put forward a comprehensive traffic management proposal which focused on the Porschestraße, the main point of entry to the city. By an irony of fate, Scharoun had to deal with the consequences of Third-Reich planning policy, as he had in Berlin in 1945. There were further parallels with Berlin in the way the planning debate was conducted in Wolfsburg, and in the repeated rejection of Scharoun's ideas.

The competition brief specified that the Porschestraße area should be linked not only spatially but also by road to the somewhat isolated Klieversberg hill.[57] Scharoun realized that it was impossible to combine both of these requirements and instead made provision for extension and reinforcement of the Porschestraße axis in order to decentralize the traffic and do away with the ring roads created by earlier planners. However it was clear even from the deliberations of the jury that traffic planning had priority over Scharoun's concept of an integrated urban plan.

The Wolfsburg traffic plan of 1963 foresaw the linking of Heinrich-Heine-Straße with the Siemensstraße by means of a major road which would create a throughway at the intersection with the Porschestraße. After the competition, the planners made rigorous attempts

H. Scharoun, Wolfsburg Theatre, model of final building, 1969.

to incorporate Scharoun's theatre into this model – but could think of nothing better than running the proposed routes through the complex, splitting it into three and so effectively robbing it of any logic.

Scharoun's proposals for Wolfsburg follow the same principles as the 1946 collective plan for Berlin.[58] They make use of existing roads, but refuse to allow the form of the inner city area to be determined by traffic requirements – as is the case in Wolfsburg today. In accordance with the competition brief, Scharoun also created an impressive city entrance in the southern area of the Porschestraße, but this has been obscured by recent urban developments. His proposal takes account of other buildings in the city centre, extending from the city hall and cultural centre out to the Köhlerberg hill. He foresaw a 'landscape' of individual buildings which emphasized the topographical conditions of the site and established a spatial connection between the Porschestraße and the Klieversberg. This approach to urban planning was the same as that of the Berlin Kulturforum. Both designs won euphoric praise from the jury; both designs were only partially realized.

Scharoun's legacy: the Kulturforum in Berlin

Scharoun's name is inextricably linked with one of the most controversial and involved chapters of German post-war history, the planning of the Berlin Kulturforum. In 1958, in his entry to the Hauptstadt Berlin competition, Scharoun had spoken of a 'spiritual band' that ran from West to East along the Spree valley.[59] One year later, he said that as a consequence of the competition: 'the large green space of Berlin, the Tiergarten, is the place to locate all the major cultural, administrative and economic sector, to reflect a sense of hierarchy.'[60] But this

Overleaf: H. Scharoun, State Library for the Prussian Cultural Heritage Foundation, Berlin-Tiergarten 1964, competition model.

thought became explicit only when the site for the Philharmonie was finalized. The initial design for the Philharmonie and auxiliary chamber-music hall shows an almost medievally closed square on axis with Stüler's Matthäi Church. The idea of a cultural forum took shape only when it was decided to build the Nationalgalerie and State Library on the same site. The project rapidly went from representing a 'spiritual band' to being a political manifesto. The continuing competition between planners in the East and West meant that the Forum grew as a response to work on the historical core of the city within East Berlin.

After winning first prize in the competition for the State Library in 1964, Scharoun took on the planning of the Forum. Here Scharoun finally had the opportunity to implement his idea of an urban landscape. The Kulturforum, through its positioning and generous scale, implied a return to a united Berlin. For Scharoun this was a positive gesture, an architectural refusal to accept the *status quo*. At the same time there were obvious weaknesses in the proposal. The individual buildings remained isolated at the edge of the Western half of the city. Scharoun did not address the mixing of functions, and the siting of the State Library at the point where the old Potsdamer Platz connected with the Landwehrkanal meant that the old fabric could not be restored if the two parts of the city were united. Scharoun also departed from his own basic principle of not allowing traffic requirements to determine planning by allowing the Forum to be dismembered by roads, in particular the West expressway and the Potsdamer Straße. Though this concession to traffic may have helped him to secure first prize in the competition, it brought into question the long-term viability of the spatial structure of the Kulturforum.

Despite the failure of his plans for Berlin in 1946 and his first major commissions such as the Kassel Theatre in 1951, Scharoun created, through his design work and theory, one of the most comprehensive conceptions of architecture in the post-war era. One weak point in this theory, however, was that Scharoun (like Häring) never made concrete, practical statements on aesthetics, but simply stated that an organic form should arise from the function and Essence of the building task. He accepted commonly founded aesthetics as well as the use of contemporary forms. The external appearance is evident from the earliest stages of the design – giving some of the buildings a formalized, over-subjective and dated look. This applies in particular to the projects of the 1950s, which dissolve externally in seemingly arbitrary details and exclude all representational and ordering elements. Scharoun realized that this was one reason why his work was misunderstood and rejected, and formulated his later projects in a much more rational and unequivocal manner. This led, at least in the case of the cultural buildings, to something like a recurrent typology – which was anathema for Scharoun. The buildings and urban plans always maintain a complex spatial and semantic relationship to the landscape and to the people who use them. But when this overall relationship is obscured by cuts or alterations, Scharoun's architecture becomes very open to attack, as illustrated by the chamber-music hall which was built after his death.

The strength, but also the weakness of Scharoun's work lies in its subjectivity – or its individuality, as Behne said in 1923. Scharoun offered solutions which responded to the individuality of human nature, in contrast to the symbols and formalism of both Modernism and Post-Modernism. From 1934 onwards, he began to evolve his own 'alternative' to Modernism, which he saw not as an easy to prescribe and replicate architectural language, but rather as an architecture which was grounded in its own time and its own place. This approach makes Scharoun's architecture much less susceptible to appropriation by a political system or power structure than a classical repertoire of forms. In 1957 Scharoun wrote prophetically that only a loss of cultural identity would lead to an adaptation of styles: 'People look for something to sustain them in face of the turbulent events of their everyday existence. If they do not find this support they flee out of their own time into an alien one. They latch onto the styles of the past and try them all out in turn. The haste with which this happens is already an indication that this process is nothing more than a preparation, a kind of emptying, to make room for the new.'[61]

Buildings and Projects

1911   Church in Bremerhaven
Design sketch

One of the earliest designs by Hans Scharoun, his competition entry for a church in Bremerhaven, was made while he was still at school. He submitted two schemes bearing the mottoes 'Everything for Love' and 'Andante' – the latter version is illustrated here. The church has a single nave and is influenced both by Jugendstil forms and by Hans Poelzig's crafts-based regionalist vocabulary. At the outset of his career, in 1910, Scharoun formulated one of the main principles of his life's work, which he expressed in this inscription below a drawing: 'An independent architect should be guided not by his feelings, but by his reflections.'

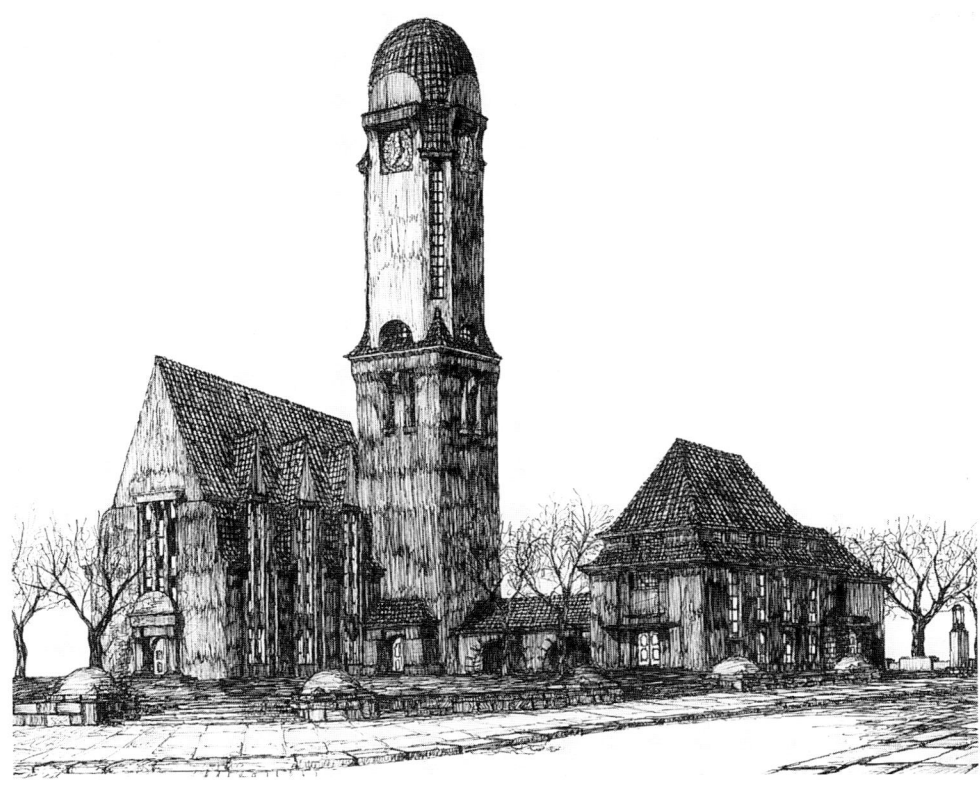

1919 Watercolours for the 'Crystal Chain'

Scharoun took part in the 'utopian exchange of letters' initiated by Bruno Taut. The correspondents called themselves the Crystal Chain. They used watercolours and drawings – there were no real building commissions in the period after the First World War – to communicate to each other their ideas and dreams of a new kind of architecture free of all earthly constraints. Scharoun wrote in one of these letters in 1919: 'Comrades in arms! We must often fight for the small things, but then the big things will, to our great joy, come to us of themselves. Everything begins with people. Everything stems from people. Through people, symbols come alive. Cosmos! A beautiful word! But if the word were unable to grow into a concept – a content – a state of being, we would be ashamed of it, of its smallness, its pettiness. We and our work are more than that. Our work is the ecstatic dream of our hot blood, multiplied by the coursing blood of millions of our fellows. Our blood is the blood of our time, our means of expressing ourselves now ... It is our desire not to speak of ways and means, but to surrender to bright colourful possibilities, to let the fantasy shine out of asceticism. We are not seeking, but storming. We want not a method of achieving a goal, but a universal goal. Infinity is not outside us: it is not a star that we can divert to earth, but something that lives within each stirring of the artist's imagination, twinkling softly.
'In creating we are gods, in understanding we are sheep. But this is how it should be. Otherwise understanding would rank above devotion, interpretation above a feverish immersion in the universe – We are still circulating blood, flowing into the gutters of alleyways and onto the Milky Way. We believe in everything (which might also be nothing, as long as it is original) and we exist!!! Otherwise we would vegetate in the mire of a conceptual botany. Hannes.'

Three watercolours for the 'Crystal Chain', 1919.

1920   Theatre, social and cultural hall, Gelsenkirchen
'Der Mensch ist gut' (People are good) competition

Scharoun ventured early into theatre design, believing that the theatre should be the most important cultural expression of a society. In the theatre/cultural centre in Gelsenkirchen, Scharoun made the massing of the building as tight as possible while linking the auditorium with the stage in order to create the effect of a unified space. The semicircular auditorium and broad stage were similar to Poelzig's 1920/21 design for the Salzburg Festspielhaus, which was much discussed at the time. In the same year, Scharoun summed up his thoughts on the theatre in his 'Ruf zum Bauen': 'Here, unconstricted by conventional theatre space, people sit between walls that have been decorated with them in mind; there, the action unfolds around the stage, ruling out alienation. The space and the action are boldly brought to the people. Form, common consciousness and common experience, in buildings, things and people, are a recurrent aspiration of our times – of Art and Life.'

Perspective of the theatre.

Ground-floor plan of the theatre.

Perspective of the complex as a whole.

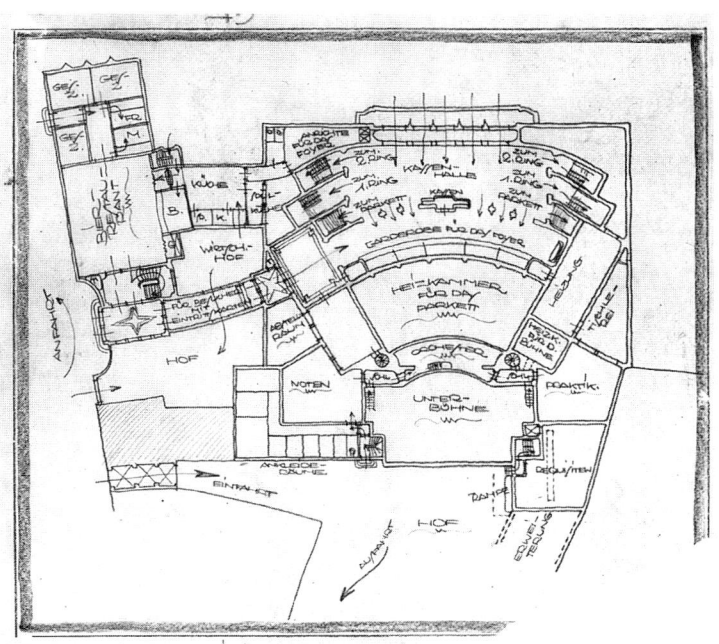

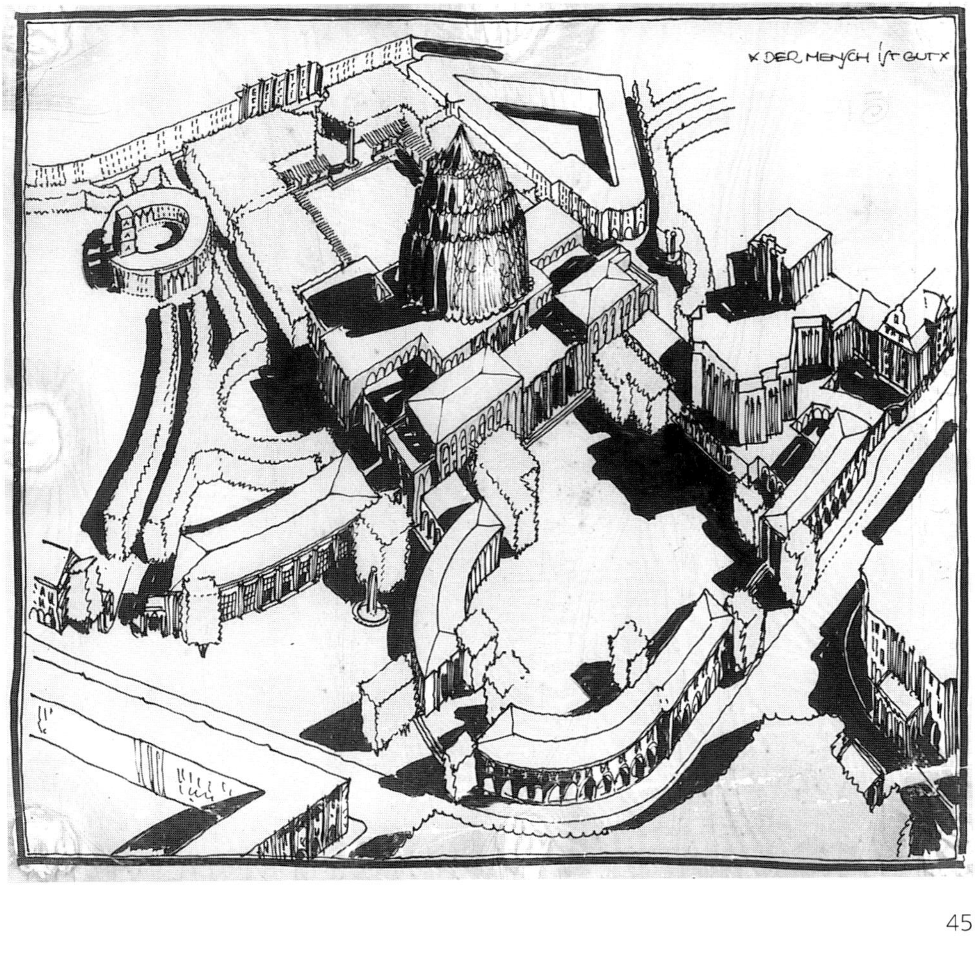

1920 Museum of Hygiene, Dresden
Entry to the 'Kultur und Zivilisation' (Culture and civilization) ideas competition

In 1911 Dresden was host to an International Exhibition of Hygiene. Its success prompted plans to build a Museum of Hygiene in the city 'to promote the idea of making the population stronger and healthier through a programme of public health care'. The museum was allocated an important urban site, on open ground behind Gottfried Semper's Opera House to the north of the Zwinger piazza by the old royal stables: the existing riding hall was to be incorporated into the new building.

In contrast to the prize-winning designs, which responded to the architectural context with Neo-Classical forms and proportions, Scharoun's museum was crystalline, Expressionist. The various spatial requirements of the programme were accommodated in a multi-winged, axially symmetrical complex which related to the Zwinger. In the centre of the complex, the main hall appears like a radiant city crown, with 16 differentiated, angular stepped façades ordered by Gothic-like vertical elements.

Perspective.

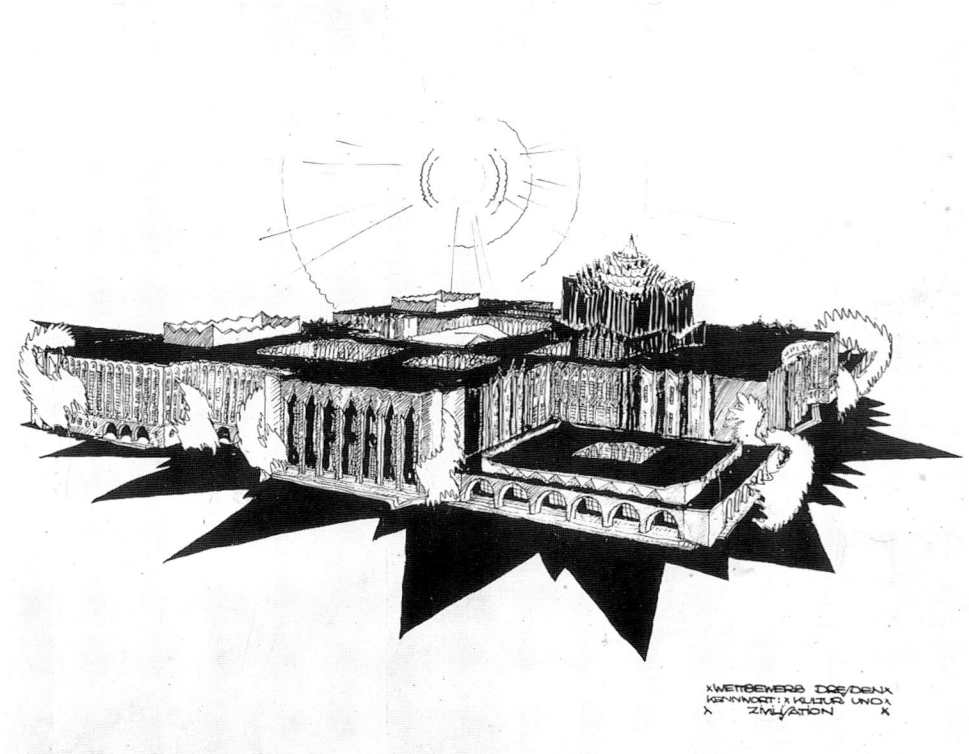

Elevation.

Plan of upper floor.

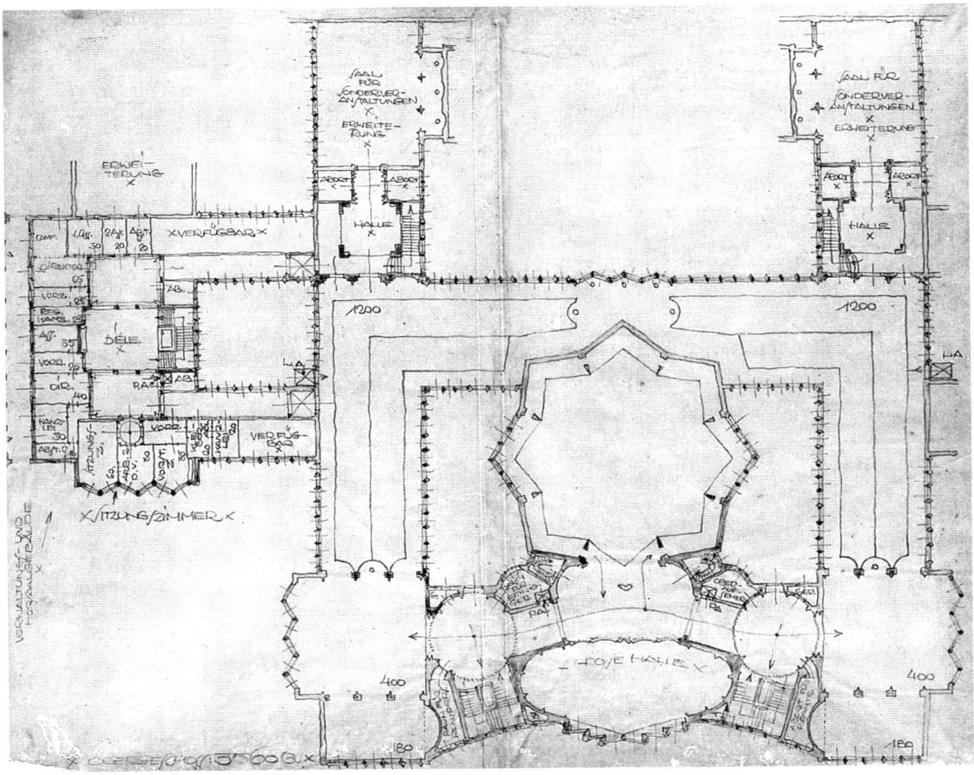

1921 Friedrichstraße high-rise, Berlin
'Innen und Aussen' (Inside and outside) competition entry

The Friedrichstraße competition was one of the most spectacular of its time. Its theme was the high-rise and, more specifically, the first skyscraper in Germany. Scharoun's entry was one of the most significant in the competition, on account of a convincing concept, unusual language of forms and individualistic graphic presentation. It adhered closely to the brief and secured the only special award from the rather academic jury. It was described by Max Berg, the city planner of Breslau, as 'one of competition's most significant achievements from an artistic point of view', its fantastic forms making it the 'most characteristic expression of the German concept of the high-rise in evidence in the competition'.

Scharoun responded to the exposed nature of the three-sided plot with three different façades which stepped back in order to bring in light and allow for the proper distance from the surrounding buildings. While these urban planning characteristics were determined by the site, the dynamic form was largely a product of a functional ordering of space. The stairwells formed glazed, vertical breaks in the façade, while the organization of the commercial spaces reinforced the horizontality of the lower part of the building. Within the presentation, the use of single-point perspective and lines denoting rays of light spelled out the link with the utopian 'people's houses' of Scharoun's contemporaries. Here, the references to Gothic architecture were of an indirect, rather ideal nature – a fashion also reflected in the Chicago Tribune Tower competition of 1922. Although the design was not drawn up in full detail, it was precisely formulated in architectural and spatial terms. The plan initially appears complicated, as is often the case with Scharoun, but it shows, for the first time, completely resolved organizational sequences, junctions and circulation.

Main elevation from the Friedrichstraße station.

Ground-floor plan.

Rear elevation.

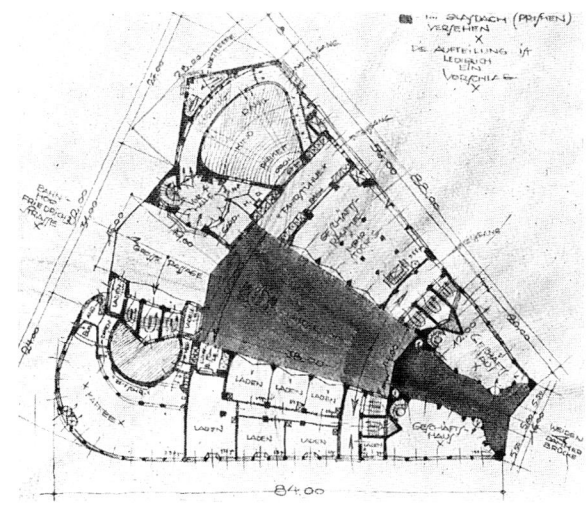

1922   Commercial building at the Börsenhof, Königsberg, Prussia
'Zeittakt' (Pulse of the times) competition entry

June 1922 saw the launch of a remarkable competition to design the largest building ever planned in Königsberg – a seven-storey commercial building with 500 offices and a modern hotel which was intended to secure the city's position as the pre-eminent trading centre in the East. The architect described the scheme in this way: 'The plan shows an open foyer that links the building with the street. The post office at the end of the entrance hall meets programmatic requirements without taking up valuable space. In the composition as a whole I have avoided a dominating order and have kept to a minimum the scale of the corridors and façades. The courtyard opens to the south, while to the north the high-rise steps back from the street. The courtyard lies at basement level and serves as a thoroughfare, giving access to car parking and the hotel grounds, from where there is a connecting path to the three parts of the hotel complex. The central part serves as a lobby: it has a glass prism ceiling which can be walked on and is accessible, in case of fire, via an iron stairway. In addition to providing accommodation for around 120 guests, the hotel has numerous well-appointed reception rooms, reflecting its intended role as a meeting place for businessmen and official visitors.'

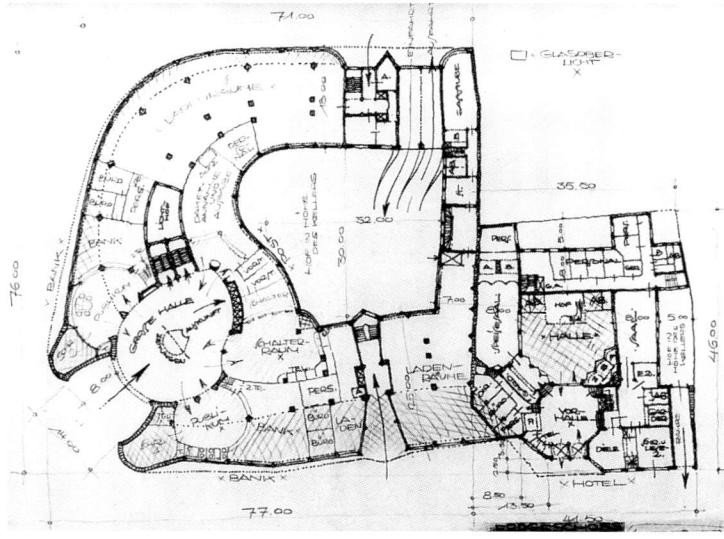

Ground-floor plan.

Right-hand page: perspective and side elevation.

1922 Chicago Tribune Tower
Competition entry

The Chicago Tribune Tower competition, launched on 10 June 1922, was one of the most spectacular international competitions of the early 1920s, attracting 264 entries. Given the prevailing taste for the Beaux-Arts in the US, it was perhaps not surprising that the 37 entrants from Germany – the largest foreign block – had little success with their modern, mostly Constructivist or Expressionist, schemes. Scharoun's own entry was not a detailed project but merely a design sketch which appears to refer directly to the work of Erich Mendelsohn, with its coarse silhouettes and its emphasis of the vertical and horizontal through the structure.

Scharoun's design caught the attention of the architectural historian Adolf Behne, who pointed to its representation of the element of movement, albeit in 'surrogate' form, and called it a phenomenon of the times. In his book *Der moderne Zweckbau*, Behne wrote: 'This work consciously incorporates its surroundings. It takes account of the "juncture which mediates between the low building and the high-rise", between the indifference of a chaotic street and a clear form. Characteristically, Scharoun has arrived at quite definite concepts of movement: "1. the façade becomes firm 2. looks for a standpoint 3. acquires tension 4. rises up and 5. carries working platforms." This could be a description of the operation of a machine. In fact, Scharoun conceives of the tower as a "machine" and not as a "house = monument". Other Functionalists also like to refer to the machine, which interests them greatly as a moving tool.'

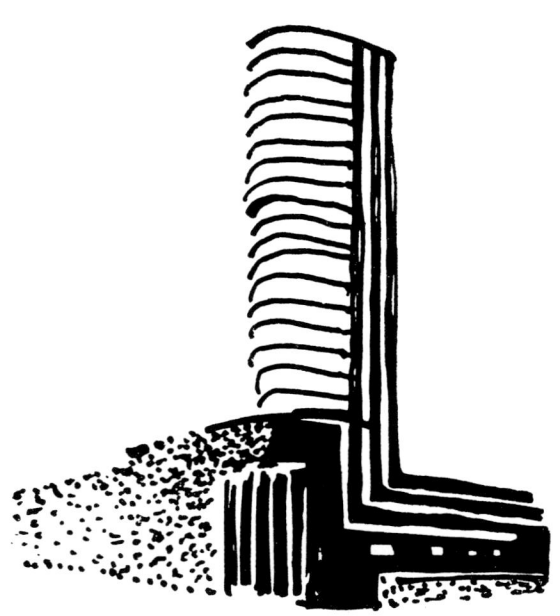

1924/25 Spa building in Bad Mergentheim
'Schweben' (Floating) competition entry

Like other works by Scharoun at the time, this design was determined paradigmatically by two factors: the building's specific location and the functional ordering of the interior. The ballroom lies to one side of an internal junction, at the centre of which is the entrance. On the other side are further small rooms, a second entrance, and finally the casino and the caretaker's quarters, which lie parallel to the street and relate to the buildings opposite. As the watercolour perspective shows, the building is dominated visually by a tall fly-tower. The broad stage and ballroom share a common axis. The cloaks, foyer storage areas are functionally related to the main rooms, and the individual spaces are expressed externally as distinct parts of the building. Scharoun's highly modern design, with its vertical and horizontal ordering elements, attracted quite a bit of attention at the time. Gustav Adolf Platz described the project in his seminal work, *Die Baukunst der neuesten Zeit* (1927), as a most eloquent example of Scharoun's spatial inventiveness, guided by the 'idea of an individual form arising from the function and the spirit of a task'.

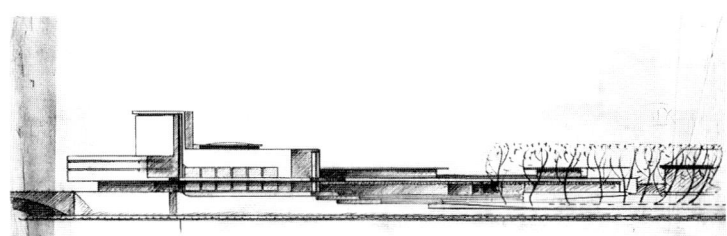

Side elevation.

Main elevation.

1925 Bochum Town Hall
'Kopf und Bauch der Stadt' (Head and belly of the city) competition entry

Scharoun attracted much attention with this clearly ordered design for the town hall of Bochum. The plan takes up the diagonal of the site; the elevation is dynamic, with graduated formal elements. Scharoun described the project in the following way: 'The starting point was to strip the municipal building of its monumentality and take it back to its essential elements, making a conscious separation between the civic part of the building and the working part, and creating a lively play of architectural form between the two halves. In fact, there are not just two, but three elements, if you include the hallway which connects the civic wing with the offices.

'The hall itself has little defining form, like the activity within it. It can be seen as an "extension of the street" (completely glazed over and between two walls) – these walls run alongside each other: one pushes forward the civic wing, and the projection is repeated to form the façade; the other wall is the starting point for the office wing. The hall gives direct access not only to the office wing but also to the intermediate public counters. The civic wing rises up organically to form a tower with a flagpole. The building masses relate directly to the street, defining it first as an external space then drawing it – half external, half internal space – into the hall. Here the office wing becomes an internal space formed parallel to the street while the civic wing rises above the street.'

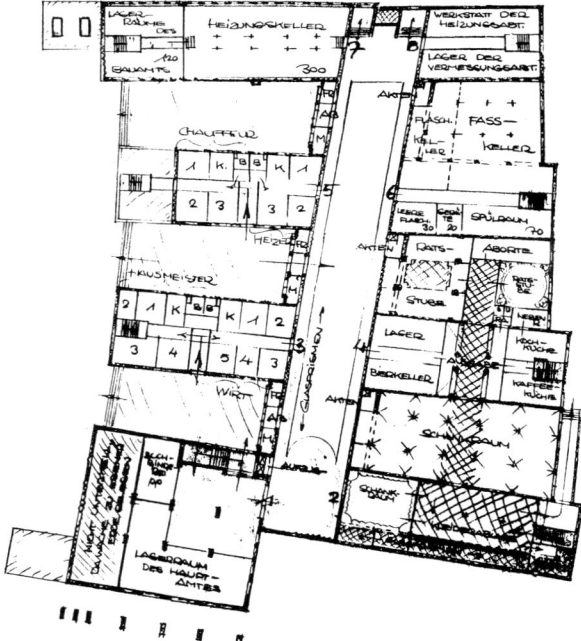

Plan at base level.

Main elevation.

Bird's eye view.

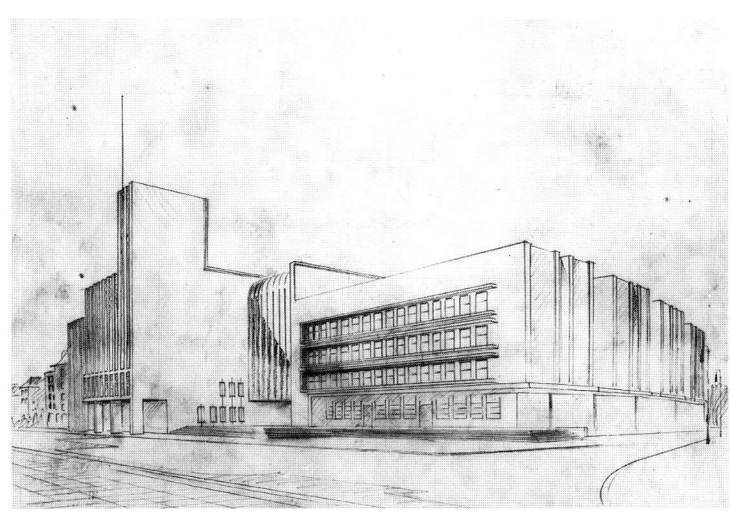

1925   Cologne bridgehead
'Zwischen Brücke und Dom' (Between the bridge and the cathedral) competition entry

The idea of creating a bridgehead on the left-hand side of the suspension bridge in Cologne was first discussed at the beginning of the 1920s. The intention was to tie together the bridge, the surrounding buildings and the nearby cathedral, taking into account the Heumarkt, one of the most important squares in the city.
In Scharoun's scheme, the bridgehead consists of two large department stores. The buildings take up the lines of the bridge, but counter its static swing with their roundness. They have an independent urban presence, accentuated by the strong horizontals and verticals in their elevations. Over on the side of the city, the new construction takes up existing building lines and is integrated with its surroundings.
With 412 entries, including works by practically all the country's well-known architects, the competition was one of the biggest held that decade. It provoked a wide debate not only on the issue of the high-rise but also on the methods of running such a large competition. Controversially, Scharoun was awarded a prize of 3000 Marks. The jury noted: 'The strong painterly quality of the design does not disguise the very modern concept underlying it. The curve of the building mass, though at first seeming unusual, forms a rhythmic link with the lines of the bridge.'

Perspective of the bridge.

Views of and from the bridge.

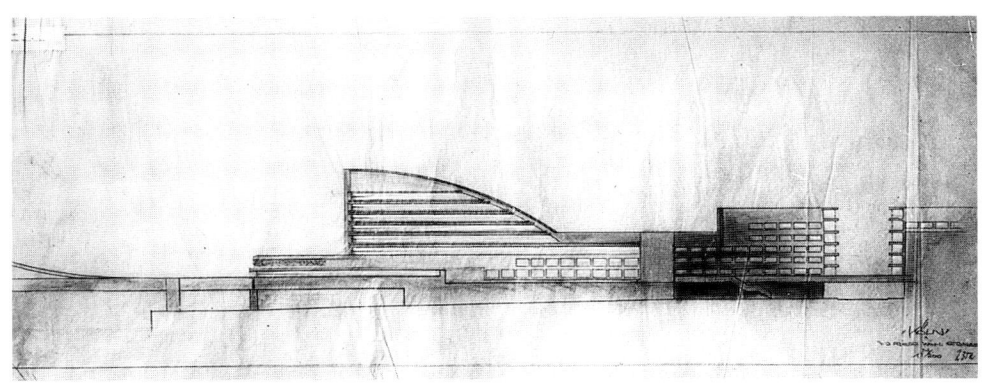

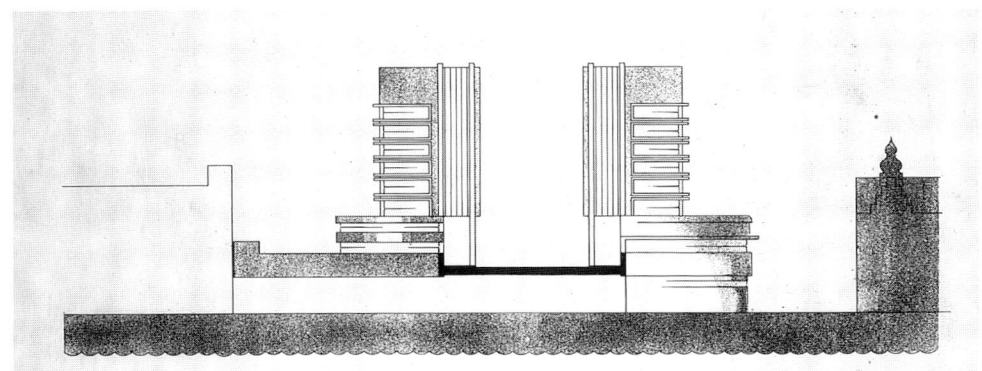

1928   Trade fair and exhibition centre, Berlin
'Spinne' (Spider) competition

The first stage of this project was a 1925 competition which established a development plan for a trade fair and exhibition centre in Berlin, clarifying traffic issues and dividing up the site to the north of the Grunewald. At the beginning of 1928 a second competition was held in anticipation of the 1930 Berlin Building Exhibition. The aim this time was to develop the scheme in accordance with a plan formulated by Martin Wagner, the city's Director of Building, and Hans Poelzig. The plan proposed an oval arrangement of the exhibition buildings to either side of a new station at the centre of the site. It also contained guidelines on the road layout, but these were not binding on the competitors as they had not yet been officially approved. The significance of the competition was reflected by the prestigious jury which included, amongst others, Paul Bonatz, Theodor Fischer, Wilhelm Kreis, Ernst May, Heinrich Tessenow and Martin Wagner.

Scharoun adhered only in part to the given conditions. He centred his design around a U-shaped high-rise hotel fronted by a concert hall. On either side were the semicircular exhibition halls which dominated the axis with the Neue Kantstraße and Kaiserdamm, the most important routes for traffic coming into the city. The plan by Wagner and Poelzig had foreseen a geometrical north-south division of the site related to developments in several nearby squares. In Scharoun's scheme, the exhibition area is screened on one side from the urban development towards the Kaiserdamm and open on the other to the parkland of Schöneberg. There is also more emphasis on the patterns and lines of movement within the site, as shown in sections of the building. Scharoun incorporated the proposed station within the trade fair, but bridged over the railway line with numerous 'spiderweb' walkways and superstructures.

This was one of Scharoun's first incursions into urban planning in Berlin. In contrast to the closed and holistic approach of most of the entrants, his proposal combines the dynamic expression of lines of movement with organic solutions that provided for future growth.

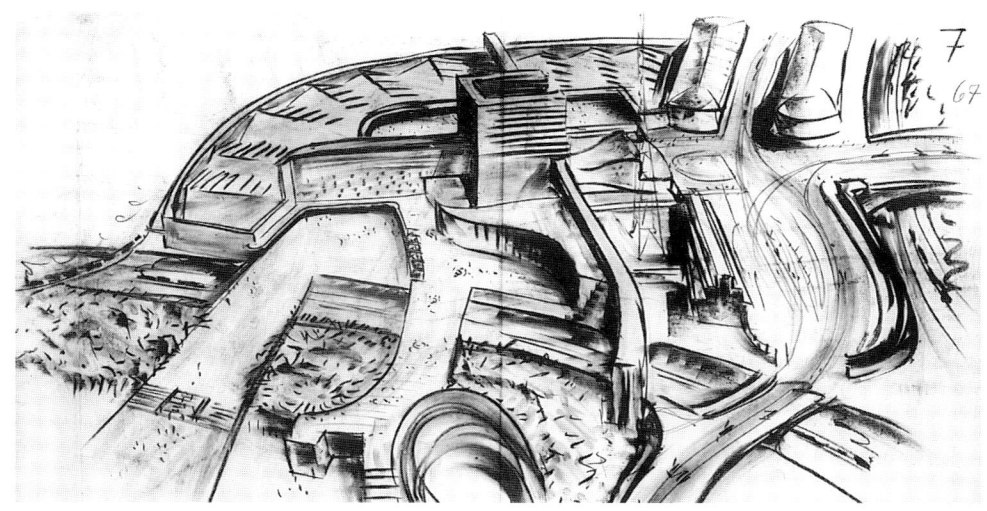

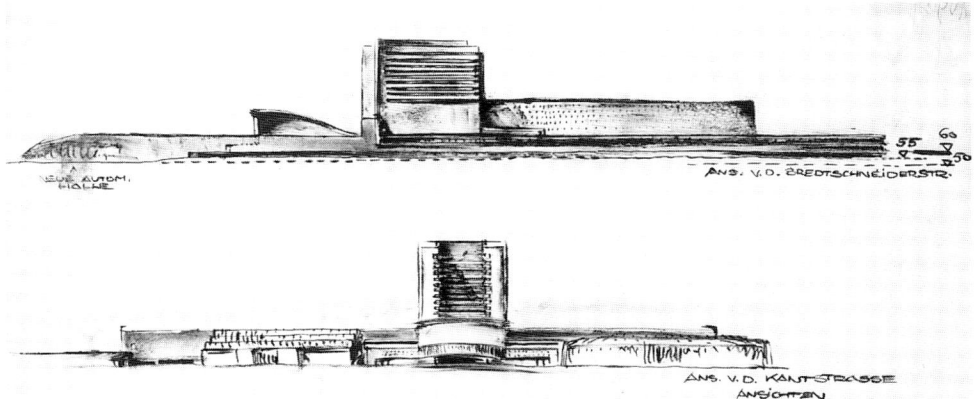

Bird's eye view from the grounds.

Views of the hotel with the concert hall.

Section through the concert hall.

1927   Transportable wooden house for the German Garden and Trades Exhibition, Liegnitz, Silesia

This wooden house was one of Scharoun's first built works. It had a biaxial plan focused around a central living area – a layout often used in later projects. The individual wall, floor and ceiling elements were standardized, allowing the rooms to be adapted to the various needs of the user.

The architect's explanatory text states: 'The house is a middle-income home for a family of four, with a special work room. The plan is determined not by a specific number of rooms, but by the question of needs. Rather than apply the usual description of a two-, three- or four-room dwelling, we should call it a dwelling for a "craftsman" or "professional" or whatever with two/four/six children, with/without servants' quarters, with/without guest accommodation.

'In response to these requirements, the house is constructed of panels which allow both internal and external flexibility. Each element of the house (living element, sleeping element, working element) is capable of being extended or rearranged. To achieve this adaptability to changing needs and locations, the external wall must itself allow a variable arrangement of the different elements of the building. This rules out "traditional" building forms. It is also important to make the house feel as spacious as possible, despite its relatively small dimensions. The practicalities of construction mean that the different parts are placed next to rather than on top of each other. The form avoids all sentimentality, being the result of an attempt to find the best possible response to the widest range of needs.

'Variations in plan and building form give new meaning to the use of wood as a construction material. Here wood is used not for its "long-established" or special aesthetic properties, but rather for its ability to permit a shifting, displacing, and re-forming.'

Right-hand page: elevation and plan.

South elevation.

O
N
S
W
SONNENBAD
ELTERN
SCHR.
KINDER
ARBEIT + SPIEL
WOHNEN
ESSEN
OFF.
TERRASSE
GED.
ARBEIT
KÜCHE
MÄDCH.
HEIZ.
WASCH
SP.
K.

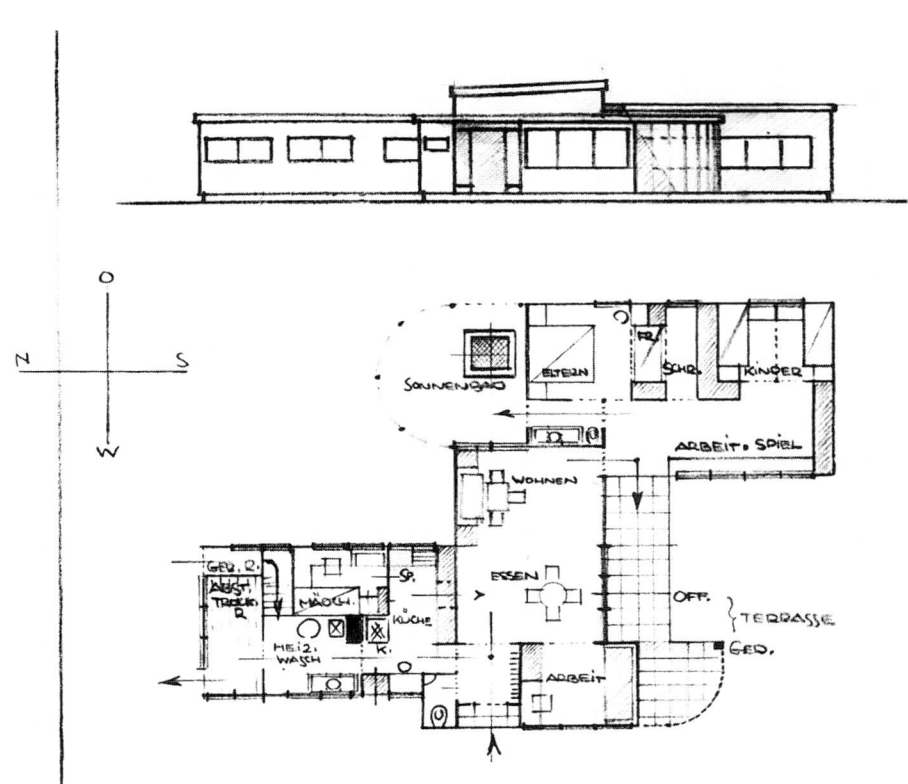

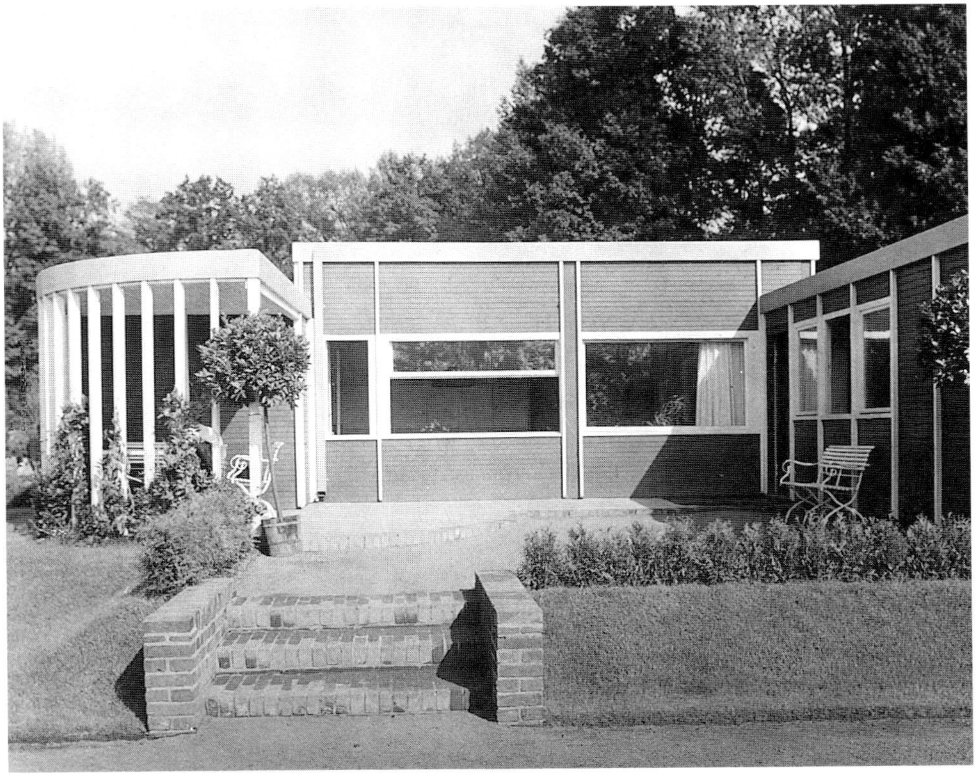

1927 Single-family house for the Werkbund Exhibition, 'Die Wohnung', Stuttgart-Weissenhof

The house designed by Hans Scharoun lies at the northeastern edge of the *Siedlung*, closing off the site along with the Peter Behrens building behind it. It is smaller than its neighbours, the terraces of Josef Frank, Mart Stam and Behrens, which step progressively upwards, following the natural slope of the site and accentuating its boundaries in keeping with Mies van der Rohe's plan. The opposite side of the *Siedlung* is marked in the same way by the houses of Le Corbusier and J. J. P. Oud.

The Scharoun house has a surface area of 107 square metres and a volume of 565 cubic metres. Construction costs totalled 48,385 Reichsmarks – making its cost per square metre (RM 85) higher than any other house on the site. The cost per cubic metre (RM 452.20) was exceeded only by Le Corbusier's semi-detached house. The rent was above average, at RM 317. The house is of dry construction, with a steel frame supporting non-structural partition panels. Some insulation is provided by rough breezeblock.

The house occupies 62 square metres of its 405 square metre site. The lower floor is ordered by a corridor which runs the length of the house, creating what Scharoun called a 'play of the line against space'. The axis leads from the entrance to the living room, separating the work areas and the living space, and continues out into the garden, where it terminates at a small pool of water. The focal point, and the largest area at around 19 square metres, is the dining room. On one side of the axis are the kitchen and the maid's room; on the other side, the rounded living area and work room. Immediately inside the entrance are the stairs to the first floor. A second entrance avoiding the living area gives direct access to the kitchen and maid's room. The living area contains few walls: Scharoun intended the rounded southern end of the house to express 'breadth, rather than the limitations of walls'. The plan is determined according to both the sequence of living spaces and their functional requirements. It is also shaped by the overall functional axis and the contrast between curves and right angles – juxtaposed both as positive and negative forms.

The upper floor covers 45 square metres and is partially set back to accommodate a large terrace over the living and dining rooms. The corridor gives onto a bathroom and three bedrooms, each with direct access to the terrace. Although the bedrooms are quite small – 10 square metres on average – they vary greatly in proportion. The shape of the bathroom is determined by the round staircase by which it is set. In drawing up the plan, Scharoun was concerned with maintaining a 'clear separation of living, sleeping and work areas'.

In contrast to the clearly ordered interior, the external form of the house appears arbitrary, with no geometric or axial determining elements. The front façade is consciously formed, while the rear façade is simple, reflecting the peripheral position of the plot. The form of the southeast side is determined by the right-angled collision of wall and roof. In contrast, the rather sculptural south and north elevations lie on the diagonal. The round garden wall in front of the right-angled eastern corner provides a further contrast. The entrance is independently expressed, marking the beginning of the axis which runs through the house. From the entrance, the staircase spirals up to the first floor, followed by a corresponding curving of the exterior. Individual formal elements articulate different living areas. The roof overhang on the upper floor, for example, extends only over the terrace, although from a functional point of view it should run the whole length of the façade. The roof of the lower floor is pulled forward over the full width of the dining room, almost to the edge of the plot. It orders the dining room and lower terrace but stops short of the rounded living area. All the windows in the house are composed in horizontal bands; the only vertical sections are the doors which, with the exception of the front door, are all fully glazed.

After many years of neglect, the house has undergone an expensive renovation which has given it a new shine.

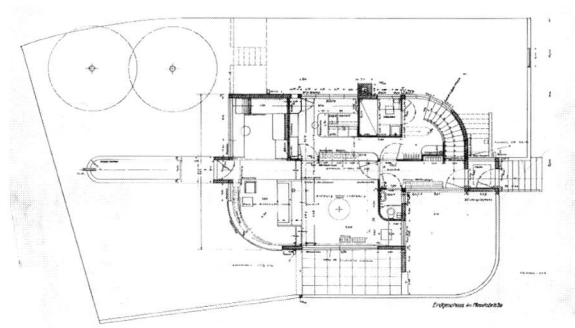

Ground-floor plan.

Northeast elevation during the exhibition.

1927 Road through the Ministry Gardens, Berlin
Planning report

In the 1920s a number of competitions focused on improving important sites in the centre of Berlin – the Potsdamer Platz, Reichstag, Platz der Republik. In conjunction with this redevelopment, there were plans to alleviate heavy westbound traffic by creating a new road which would connect the Französische Straße with the Jägerstraße south of the Potsdamer Platz. This scheme was dependent on the relocation of government ministries to the Spreebogen area, as the proposed road ran through the Ministry Gardens. Martin Wagner, the Director of Building in Berlin, commissioned Peter Behrens, Hans Poelzig, Adolf Rading, Hans Scharoun and Heinrich Tessenow to prepare a report. The results were shown in a 'Special Exhibition of Urban Planning Projects' organized by the Ring Group as part of the 1927 'Greater Berlin Art Exhibition'.

Scharoun proposed a number of options, including one which preserved the gardens by placing the road in a glass tunnel. In the version illustrated here, the line of the road is the prime element of the urban plan. Two elongated five-storey buildings flank the curve of the new street and form an architectonic corridor which not only obscures the old buildings but also creates hard-to-deal-with residual spaces. Hugo Häring appositely observed that Scharoun '... carved the traffic route cleanly out of the blocks of buildings, making the street frontage the channel for the stream of traffic'.

The proposed new road was also intended to serve an enlarged commercial area in the western part of the city. However, like most of the ambitious plans for redeveloping the city initiated by Martin Wagner, the proposed road through the Ministry Gardens never materialized, in this case primarily because of the obdurate resistance of the ministers.

Model showing the construction over the Französische Straße.

Variant without gate building.

Curved street frontage at the junction of Jäger-straße and Französische Straße, with gate building.

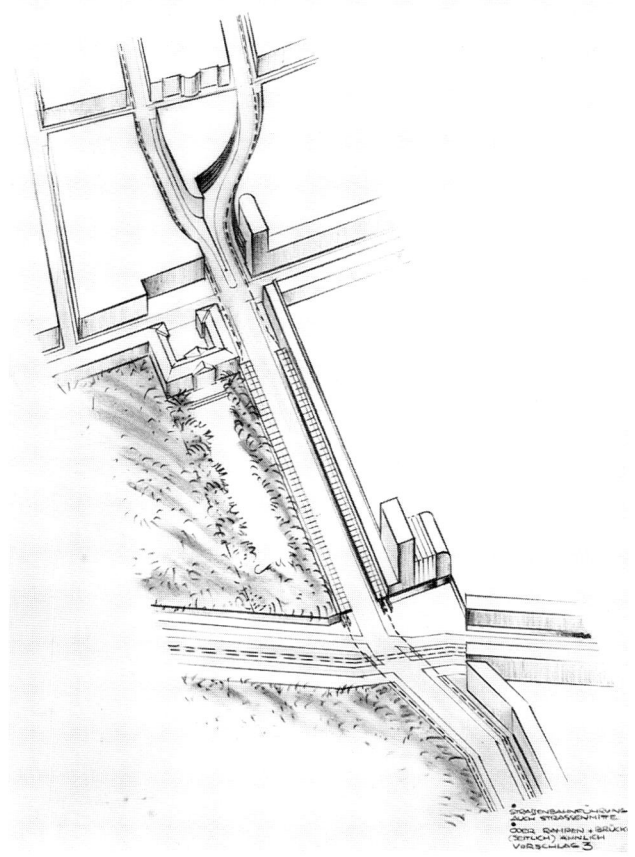

1927   Extension of the Reichstag building, Berlin
'Balance' competition entry

There were 278 entries to the August 1927 open competition to design an extension to the Reichstag. The difficulty of adding to Wallot's formally complete building was illustrated by the fact that the most popular solution was for a separate new building linked to the old one via a bridge. Scharoun proposed a bridge-like superstructure, conceived as an autonomous building containing a variety of functions, spanning the road on the north side of the Reichstag towards the River Spree.

In his explanatory text, Scharoun wrote: 'The key word "balance" was chosen because it was necessary to establish a visual link between the two formal parts – the bridge and building – and the massive corner towers, while ensuring that the bridging-over did not restrict circulation. My solution is not to create a counterpoint to the Reichstag and then link the two buildings via a visually subordinate bridge, but to make a four-storey raised linking structure which has the presence of a building.

'To complement the desired monumental effect of the Reichstag building, the new extension is as elegant, light and reticent as possible. The connecting building is constructed in the same manner as a "bridge", with frame supports extending the whole height of the building just behind the non-structural façade. This modern system of construction eliminates the need for any additions that might counteract the impression of lightness, such as concrete lintels, wall arches, etc. . . . .'

Proposal showing the road leading directly to the Reichstag.

Variants with curved road.

1928 Schlichtallee group of schools, Berlin-Lichtenberg
'Entwicklung' (Development) competition design

The complex is arranged in three distinct parts: a grammar school, middle school and vocational school, with administrative rooms and common facilities in between. It consists primarily of long rectangular blocks, placed at right angles to each other. In his project description, Scharoun said that the design derived from the specific characteristics of the site: '... [it] results from the elongated nature of the site, with its dominant east-west axis connecting – to the west – with existing buildings.' Despite these words, the complex barely takes account of the existing buildings. There was a second imperative: 'to orientate the classrooms, that is the individual school buildings, north-south (in contrast to the east-west axis mentioned above).' Here Scharoun's prime concern was the form of the complex as a whole; there is no evidence of the organic-functional ordering of classrooms and common rooms that marked his later school designs.

The project is wholly in the spirit of abstract German Functionalism, and may be compared in some ways with the Bauhaus building in Dessau designed by Walter Gropius in 1926. In both schemes the functional units – the individual blocks – consist of flat-roofed rectangular solids which are interpenetrated at lower levels by orthogonally arranged corridors or passageways in order to form the building as a whole. In the Bauhaus the administrative area spans the road on *pilotis,* linking the different blocks. At Schlichtallee, Scharoun does the same thing, placing the administrative area over the passageways diametrically opposite the entrance.

Elevation.

Isometric.

Ground-floor plan.

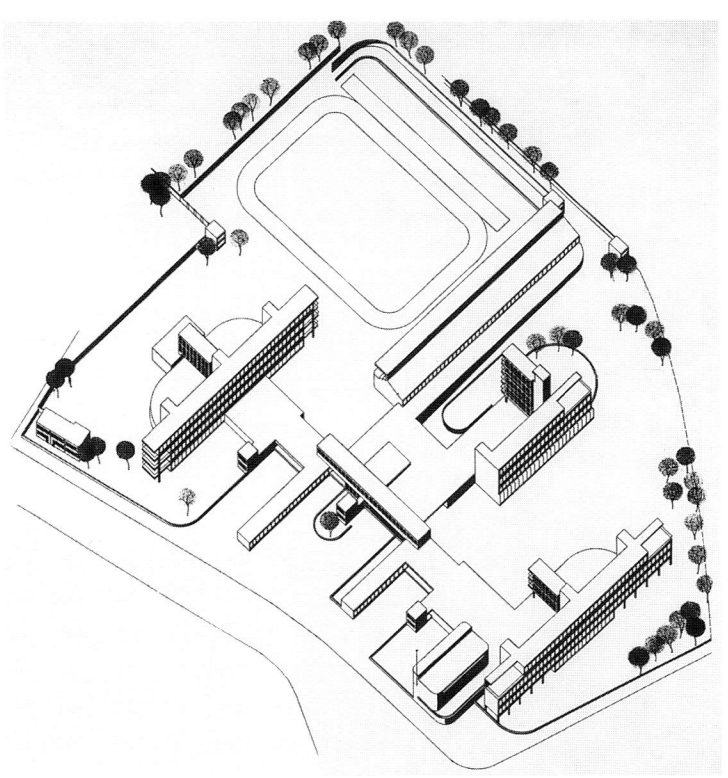

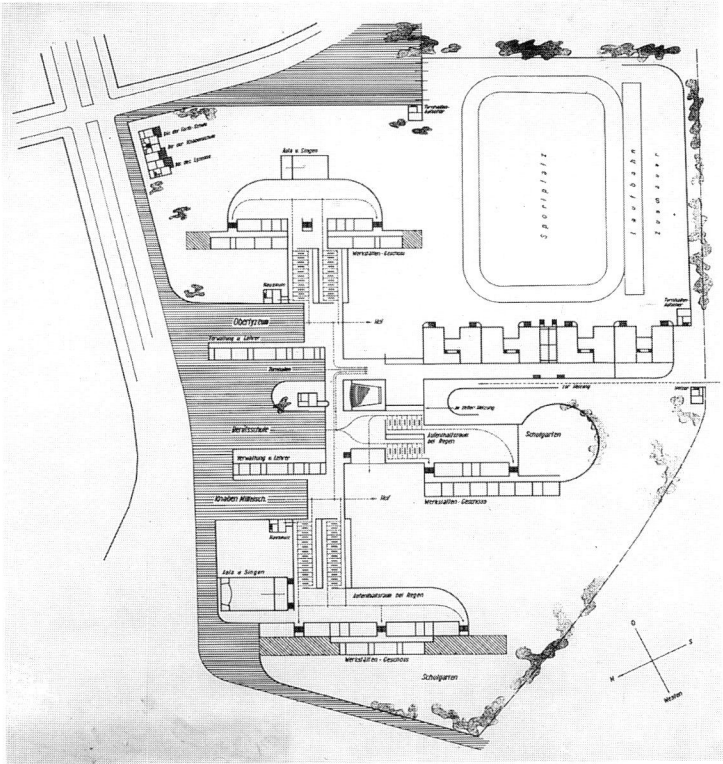

1928/29 Apartment building on the Kaiserdamm, Berlin-Charlottenburg

The Kaiserdamm housing was designed while Scharoun was still teaching at the Academy in Breslau. It represented not only his first built work in Berlin, but also his first experience of designing apartments. The impetus for the scheme came from the Jacobowitz Construction Company, which was financing apartment houses before it was common practice to do so. The construction of the apartments coincided with the building of the first large *Siedlungen* in Berlin: this was a time when housing design was dominated by the issues of the 'minimum existence' dwelling and accommodation for single people.

The building contains one- and two-room apartments for single people or couples. The interiors were designed not by Scharoun, but by Georg Jacobowitz of the construction company. Unusually, Scharoun's involvement was limited to the external appearance — which became a virtuoso exercise. Even at the time, the building attracted a good deal of attention, with its oval side windows, transposed staircase windows, dynamic corner solutions and deliberate use of colourful details. The result is one of the New Architecture's most successful façades, which has lost none of its quality over the years.

Perspective.

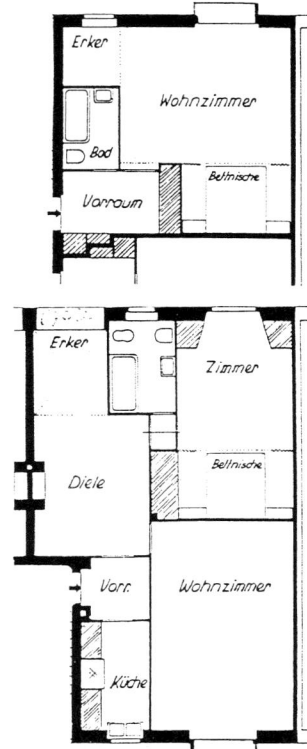

Plans of one- and two-room apartments.

View from the Kaiserdamm.

1929 Housing block for the Werkbund Exhibition, 'Wohnung und Werkraum', Breslau

In the housing block for the Werkbund Exhibition in Breslau we can see for the first time a number of elements which Scharoun was to develop fully in later projects. The elongated building is divided into three parts. At either end are parallel wings – one containing one-room apartments, the other two-room apartments. The wings are linked to each other by a diagonal containing the common spaces such as the hall, restaurant and terrace. Here for the first time Scharoun divided the mass of the building functionally and made a formal distinction between the purely functional rooms and the public or common facilities. The central area of the building effectively becomes a separate formal study, with projecting walls, curved paths and decklike roofs. A contemporary critic noted a tendency towards 'questionable artistry'.

The internal planning caused a particular furore. In order to make two floors accessible from a single corridor, the two-room apartments were set over three levels, resulting in relatively small, scattered rooms and a lack of privacy. The arrangement of the site, which at first appears arbitrary, is in fact ordered very exactly with regard to the various functions. The two blocks of housing are orientated to the southwest: the wing with one-room apartments shields the grounds from the street and joins with the diagonal of common rooms to form an enclosed garden area on the interior. To the rear the common areas relate to the park behind the building, while to the front they open onto the rest of the *Siedlung*. The technique of diagonally shifting individual building parts relative to each other arose from the given site, but was also applied formally by Scharoun to order the design and make it dynamic – not only in this scheme but in many subsequent designs. Of all the buildings in the *Siedlung*, only those of Scharoun and Adolf Rading were deemed to have 'atypical formal conceptions'. In 1929 Ludwig Hilberseimer wrote that only Scharoun's block went 'beyond the framework of its setting', alluding to the innovative planning of the smaller apartments. The double stacking of the two-room apartments around one corridor dispensed with the need for an intermediate landing. The placing of living room and bedroom behind each other with the bathroom in between enabled not only good lighting but through ventilation and at the same time economized on façade exposure.

The housing block in Breslau was Scharoun's first large-scale building project. As critics have pointed out, the asymmetrical plan was hardly determined by function. At this stage, many decisions were taken intuitively and only rationalized much later. In 1928 Scharoun wrote: 'Until we in Germany advance to a state of awareness capable of replacing our "national mindset", intuition must repeatedly serve as a moving force.'

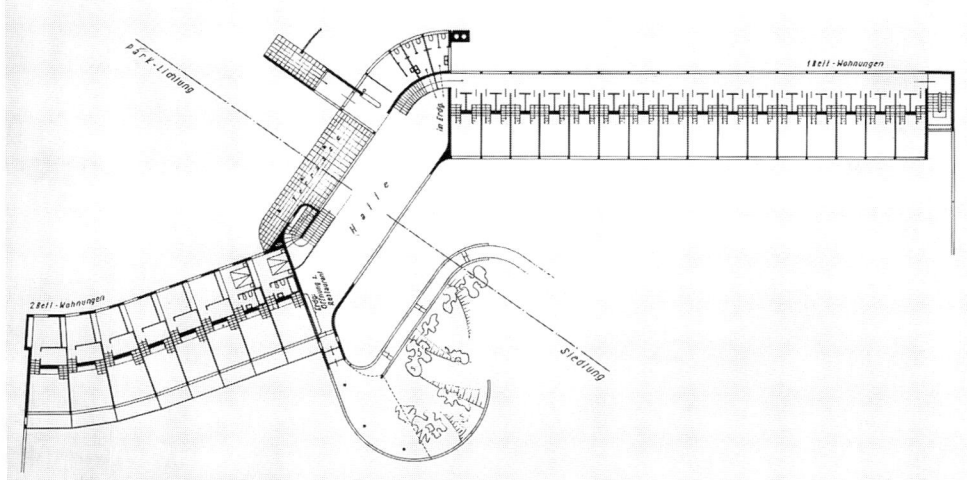

Main elevation of the *Siedlung*.

Ground-floor plan.

Section and apartment plans. The section shows the stepping of the apartments, which are accessible from only one corridor.

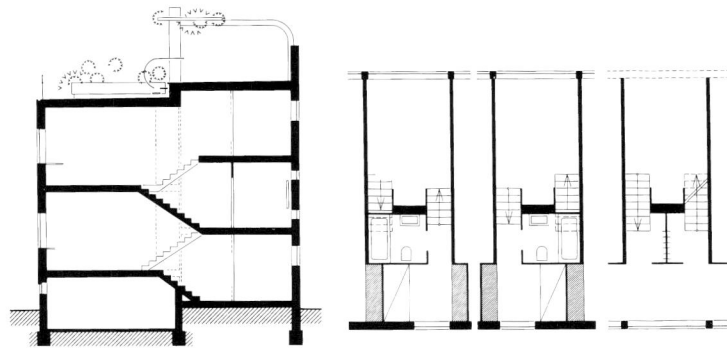

1929/30 Apartment building on the Hohenzollerndamm, Berlin-Wilmersdorf

The apartment building on the Hohenzollerndamm. like the one on the Kaiserdamm, was planned by Georg Jacobowitz, with Scharoun designing only the façades. The apartments here are larger: there are one- and two-room units with sub-dividable hallways, as well as apartments with an additional smaller room. While the façade repeats some of the detailing of the Kaiserdamm building, it is on the whole more reticent. The windows have a stronger horizontal effect while the corner at the Hohenzollerndamm and Mansfelderstraße is emphasized with rounded balconies that pick up the dynamic formal vocabulary of Erich Mendelsohn.

In 1932 Scharoun wrote in *Bauwelt*: 'The housing on the Hohenzollerndamm was designed in 1929/30 with the benefit of experience gained with the Kaiserdamm block. In the two-room apartments, both rooms have sleeping niches, while the living rooms are of varying size. Excellent natural lighting is ensured by the elongated lightwells, which run from stair to stair. The block therefore really consists of two rows placed parallel to each other on either side of the lightwells and staircases. Alternate floor levels are accessible from the half-landing. This height differential means that although six apartments give onto the stairs on each storey the corridors don't look like barracks. On the upper floor of the rear row there are studios. The courtyard has a basement to accommodate cars.

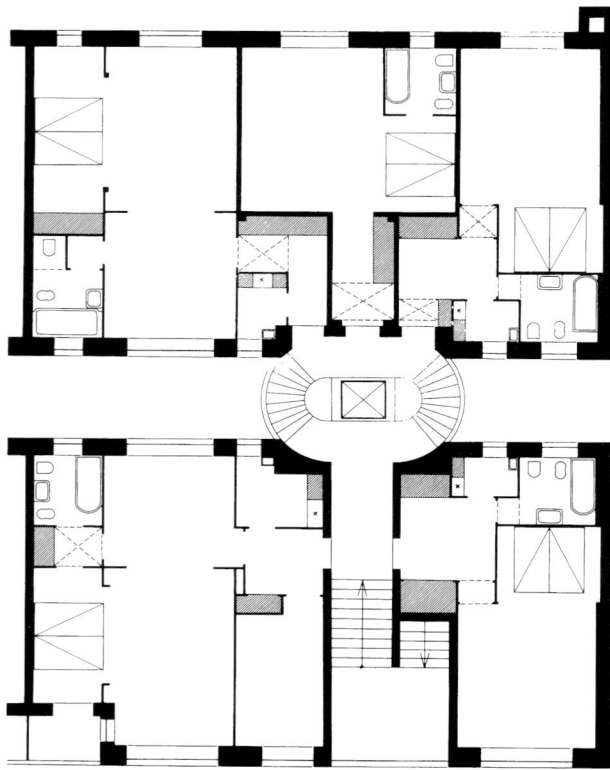

Apartment plans.

Right-hand page: view from the Hohenzollerndamm.

1930 Siemensstadt *Siedlung*, site plan and housing, Berlin

The Siemensstadt *Siedlung* was the largest project that Scharoun undertook before the war. Although it was located in the Charlottenburg area, near the Siemens factory, it was not specifically designed for the workers there, as is often assumed. The scheme was commissioned by the Berlin-Heerstraße cooperative housing association, which asked a number of architects to propose a development plan: Walter Gropius, Otto Bartning, Hugo Häring, Hans Scharoun, Fred Forbat and Paul Rudolf Henning – all of them, bar the last two, members of the Ring Group. Scharoun's plan was deemed the best by the group and was built. Scharoun combined the favoured model for mass housing at the time – the terrace – with his spatial interests, including the relationship between internal and external space. The southern part of the site contained established trees which Scharoun wanted to preserve and was divided in two by roads (the Jungfernheideweg and Mäckeritzstraße) and a curved railway embankment. Scharoun's housing is the first you see when you go through the V-shaped entrance to the *Siedlung*, and it has effectively become its trademark. It presents a right-angled, graduated façade with strong rows of windows and curved projecting balconies. Popularly known as the 'armoured cruiser', it is indeed reminiscent of a nautical superstructure, with its rounded roof terraces and decklike balconies. The section of the building that curves round the Mäckeritzstraße to close off the *Siedlung* has succinct projecting stairwells hanging from seemingly unsupported balconies. The internal planning is also unconventional. The two-and-a-half room apartments are not simply arranged but interlocking so that one living room overlooks the street, the next one the garden.

Model of the *Siedlung*.

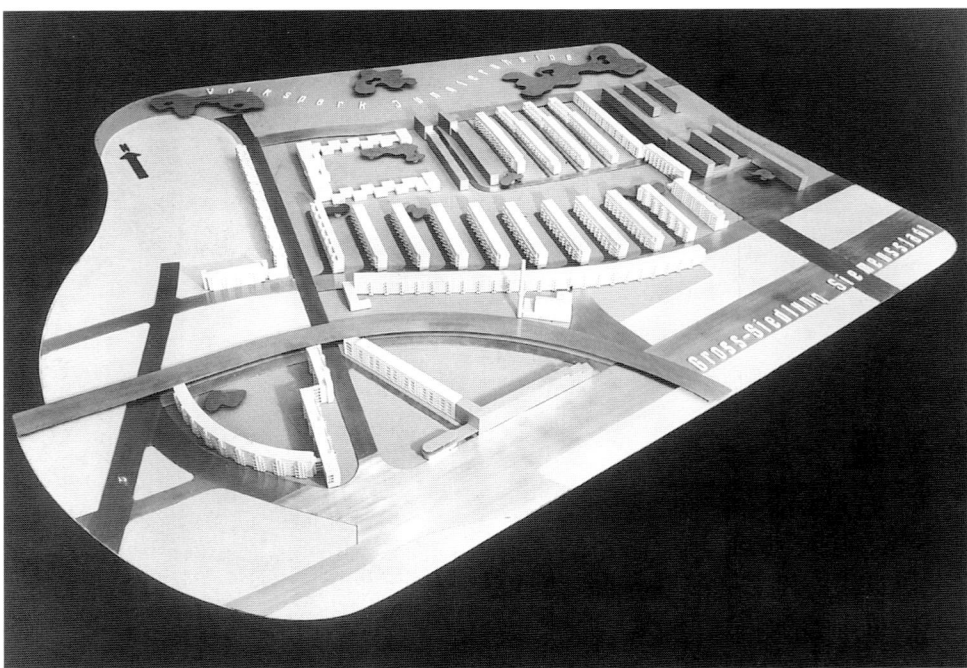

Facing this, the other terrace of housing presents a deliberate contrast, with a considerably more restrained façade and wide loggias. But behind this simpler façade are some 66-square-metre, two-and-a-half room apartments which are among the best thought-out solutions of the New Architecture. Extending the full length of these apartments is a central living area, which forms almost a 'room in the middle', flanked by the loggia and the open dining area. There are small dividing areas between the bathroom and bedroom and the entrance and kitchen. The apartments provided the maximum amount of comfort in the minimum space. It is rare for architects to live in social housing they have themselves designed – but Scharoun lived in one of these apartments for a long time.

The 'armoured cruiser' on the Jungfernheideweg.

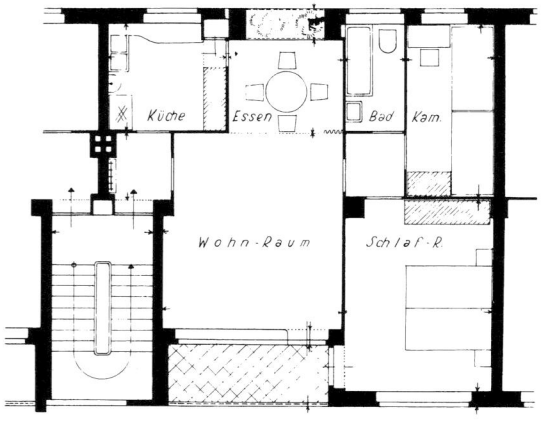

Living room in the two-and-a-half-room apartment, Jungfernheideweg.

Plan of the same apartment type, 66-square-metres.

Skewed plan of the two-and-a-half-room apartments in the 'armoured cruiser'.

Right-hand page: houses on the Mäckeritzstraße with projecting stairwells and balconies.

1932   Gustav-Adolf Memorial Church, Breslau-Zimpel
Competition entry

From 1925 to 1932 Scharoun was a full professor at the State Academy for Fine and Applied Arts in Breslau, Silesia. This period was, in his own words, a 'springboard to Berlin', providing the opportunity to work on many projects besides the housing for the Werkbund Exhibition. Scharoun's last competition in Silesia was for a Protestant church in Breslau-Zimpel in 1932. That same year, the Academy was closed down by Brüning's special decree.

The church has an axial, symmetrical U-shaped plan with a central bell tower. It is divided into three in the manner of a basilica and has narrow, top-lit side aisles. The modulated lighting, the considered spatial ordering and the skilful linking of the traditional church space with contemporary form combined to bring subtle innovations to the genre of modern church building.

West elevation.

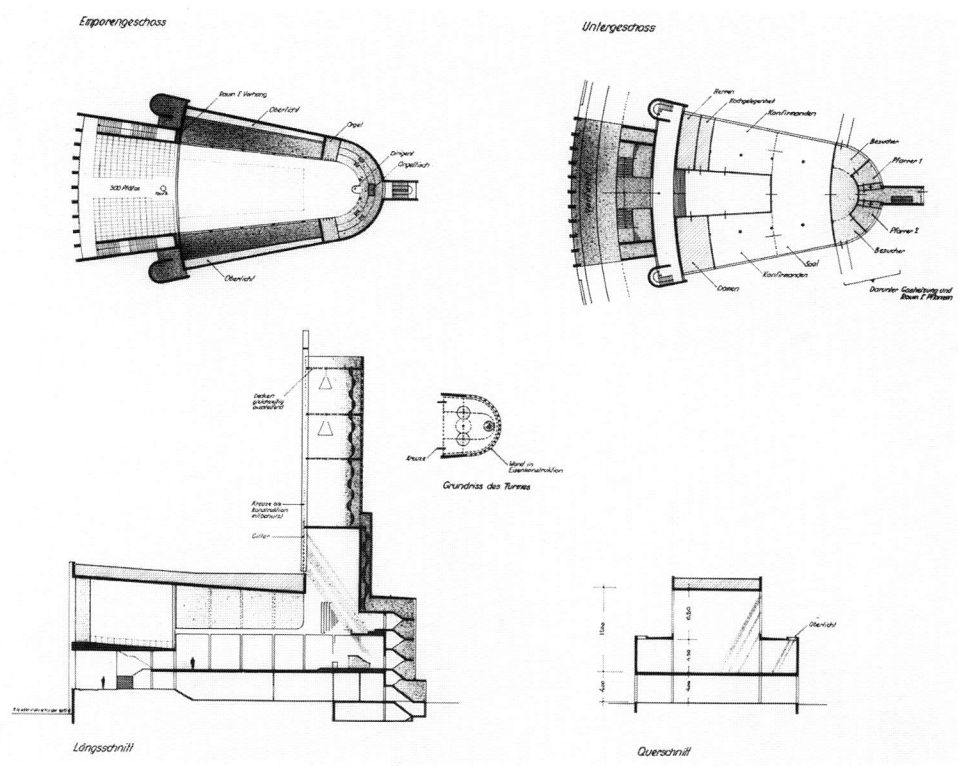

Plans and sections.

Southwest elevation.

1932 'The growing house' – a wooden house for the 'Sun, Light and Housing for All' Exhibition (Sonne, Licht und Haus für alle), Berlin

'Sun, Light and Housing for All' was organized by Berlin's Director of Building, Martin Wagner, and shown in the Berlin Trade Fair Halls in 1932. The exhibition included selected projects from a limited competition to design a 'growing house', also initiated by Wagner. The competition was intended to respond to the changed lifestyles of the future, when it was anticipated that joblessness would force more and more people to live in small, simple houses on the edge of the city in colonies centred around allotments. The house of the future was also conceived as being more rational, pre-fabricated, extendable and, if a work opportunity demanded it, demountable.

Developing the construction techniques he had used in his transportable wooden house for the German Garden and Trades Exhibition in Liegnitz in 1927, Scharoun devised a system of construction that allowed the house to grow, in sections, from a single space of 20 square metres to a four-room house with 60 square metres of usable space.

In his explanatory text, the architect wrote: '... The rapid, comprehensive development of a standardized type in the rented housing sector has simply not been paralleled in the area of the single-family house. This market requires investment of the client's own time and money, making it unsuitable for mass production. Perhaps the solution here is a modular system, adapted to modern fabrication methods and taking account of the client's wishes as well as legitimate public interests.

'The modular system is developed from techniques of furniture manufacture; the factory-produced building elements constitute the modular unit.

'The assembly-line manufacture of the elements determines the standardized price per module.

'The building unit here is considerably smaller than the "section", "core", "extended core", etc., that generally form the basis of a "growing house" project.

'This division of larger units into smaller ones allows industrial production while taking into account the wishes of the individual client. It also permits elements to be reused or rearranged at a later date to form a completely new house.

The house during the exhibition.

'But perhaps the most important thing is that the modular system enables the client to look at the drawings at any time during the design process and see how much the building will cost (assuming the standardization of internal fittings).

'Thus the client gains direct experience of the conflict between what he wants and what his money can buy, giving him a real grasp of what can be achieved, of what the priorities should be. The client is drawn directly into the process of creating his home.

'The device for matching up industrially produced building elements with individual desires is a catalogue – which plays as important a role as the bearer and medium of ideas as the practical realization of the various parts of the construction process itself . . .

'The house at this exhibition is of wood construction. The external wall consists of a lapped-board timber cladding over bituminous roofing felt and timber subframing with an air space. The inner face consists of Solomit lining felt and Celotex panels. The wall panels are load-bearing. The walls are strengthened with external and internal wall-ties which are fixed to each other and the panels to form a T-shaped support linked with the vertical pieces of the frame. The wall is intended to combine the best insulating properties with the greatest lightness and to express this lightness clearly in its form . . .'

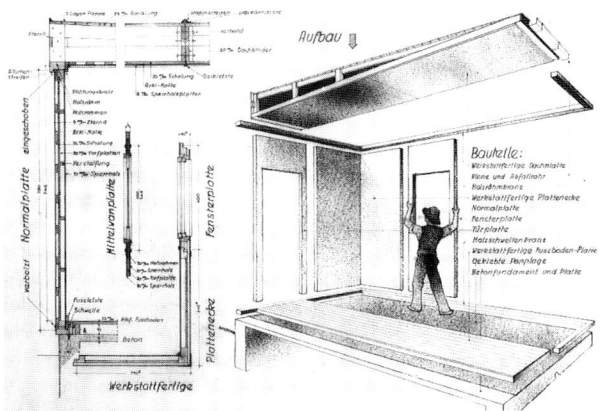

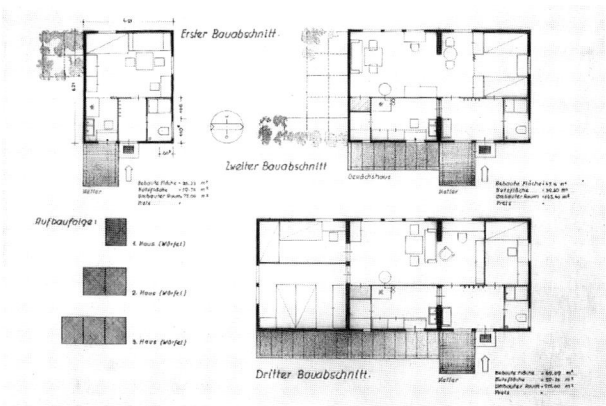

The construction principle of the growing house.

1933   Schminke House, Löbau, Saxony

Fritz Schminke – the owner of a pasta factory in Löbau – invited both Hans Poelzig and Scharoun to design a villa behind his factory. Scharoun took up the commission and designed what was not only his finest but also his most expansive single-family house of the pre-war period. The conditions were near perfect: the site was large and the architect was given a great deal of creative and financial freedom. The house has a clearly expressed functional dynamic. Contemporary photographs show a nautical streamlining accentuated by the pool (designed by landscape architect Herta Hammerbecher) in front of the gable end. For Scharoun, however, the nautical link lay not so much in the external appearance as in the construction. The house had an independent steel frame similar in profile to those used in shipbuilding.

Typically, Scharoun developed the design in response to the difficult topography of the site. The plot faces north, giving rise to an elongated plan in which the rooms on the long sides share a double aspect. The corners are rotated 30 degrees – towards the south at the front and the north at the back. This dual axis creates unusual spatial structures. The interpenetrating living spaces appear to rise naturally out of their functions and the surrounding landscape. On entering the house, the visitor is drawn by the spatial arrangement into the living area. Though the idea of a dual axis underlies the house, Scharoun does not allow it to become an over-riding geometric principle. When the space requires it, he breaks through the grid. Similarly, the spatial element does not remain unchallenged: the dining room simply pushes out of the façade, to create more space inside. The sharp angle of the terrace runs counter to the edge of the roof, while the diagonal external stair offsets the horizontality of the three levels.

The eastern part of the house is almost completely glazed to form a 'summer room'. This continues into a small conservatory which achieves maximum light with a skewed glass wall. Julius Posener was quick to recognize the importance of the house, which he described in 1935 as 'one of the most subtle architectural works of our time'. The Schminke House is an important step towards organic-functional building. The arrangement of space is ordered not by a geometric principle – not by the primacy of a right angle or cube – but by a functional sequence.

The conservatory on the northeast side of the house.

South elevation.

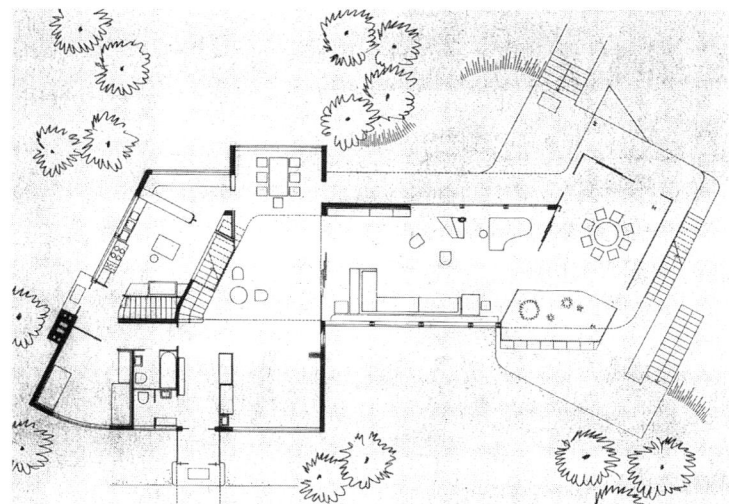

Ground-floor plan.

Overleaf: northeast elevation of the house shortly after completion.

1933 Mattern House, Bornim, near Potsdam

Between 1934 and 1945 Scharoun was excluded from all large projects and came to depend on private clients, who provided him with the opportunity to build around 20 smaller works.

There seems to be a change in Scharoun's architecture around 1933/34, with Hitler's coming to power. Many observers have described this as a 'shift to the organic'. These projects arose, in Scharoun's own words, 'under difficult circumstances', yet their plans are often freer and more functional in an organic sense than those of earlier works. The small, L-shaped house for the landscape designer Hermann Mattern represents a first step towards a 'dissolved' plan. The decisive innovation is that the basically orthogonal plan is disrupted by the west wall in the living room, which curves in towards the terrace door, creating a small, limited partition between the continuous living and dining area. The intrusion of the wall into a simple, rectangular space defines separate spaces and relationships. It gives rise to a functional space, or, as Adolf Behne put it, a space representing 'a will and concept'. The line of the wall appears arbitrary and formless, as if it were merely an imaginary movement. The curve of the wall accommodates a sofa designed specifically for the spot. Here we have early evidence of an organic spatial movement, a secondary geometrical form. At the same time the external form of the spaces corresponds exactly to their internal expression. This change took place in stages; it was not yet a general principle of Scharoun's work.

In 1936 Oskar Schlemmer decorated the house with a mural that relates to the round window of the dining room. Hermann Mattern designed the garden for this house and for many of Scharoun's later commissions.

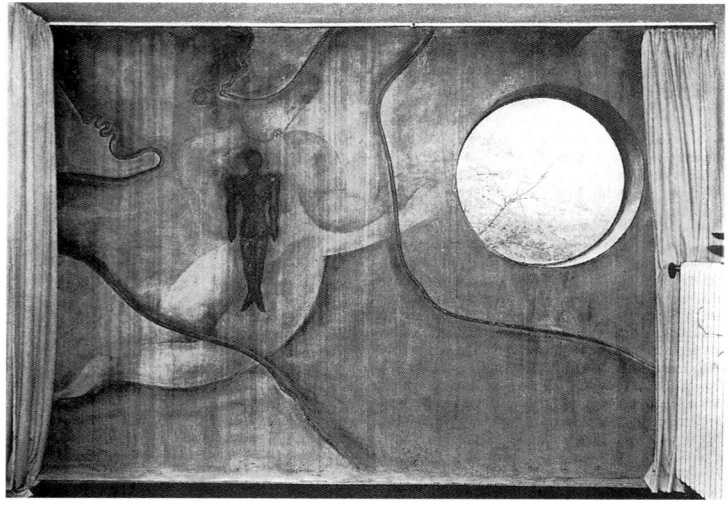

Mural by Oskar Schlemmer.

Ground-floor plan and section.

The open workroom of the house.

Southwest elevation.

1934 Holiday houses for a hotel in Vitznau, Switzerland

Vitznau is a small town on Lake Lucerne, at the foot of the Rigi mountain in central Switzerland. Scharoun collaborated with the Lucerne architect Hanns Hirt on the design of homes for year-round or holiday use on a 33,000 square metre site, which included the Hotel Bellevue. The homes were intended to take full advantage of the site and views over the lake. As Scharoun said in May 1934: 'The unique, forceful landscape and rich vegetation give rise to a solution tied to the landscape, in which the terraces and the elongated promenades form colourful counterpoints to the rich, domestic-scale gardens around the houses and the natural elements of the mountainside.' To help achieve this goal, Scharoun turned to the landscape architect Hermann Mattern, for whom he had just built a house in Bornim.

Scharoun proposed a stepped, three-storey house type, with the entrance, kitchen and dining room on the ground floor; a living area and large terrace on the first floor; and bedrooms above. As required by the programme, the building is orientated towards the lake with projecting terraces and long verandas. The project was intended to advertise the quality of German architecture and landscape design abroad, thus, it was hoped, attracting German purchasers. However this was not to be, as it was becoming increasingly difficult for Germans to invest abroad, and the project was abandoned.

Perspective with view of Lake Lucerne.

Plans of the main and base level.

Elevation.

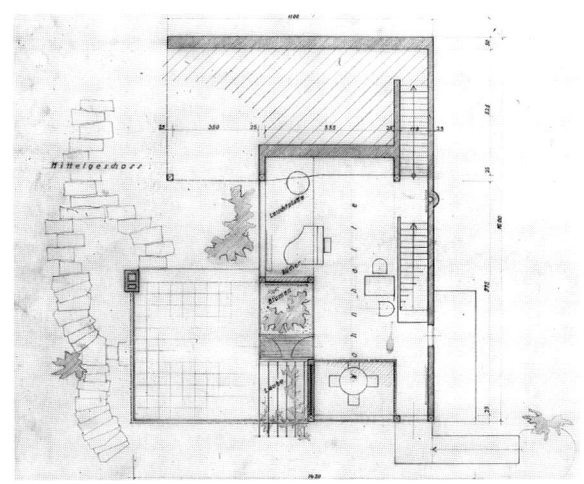

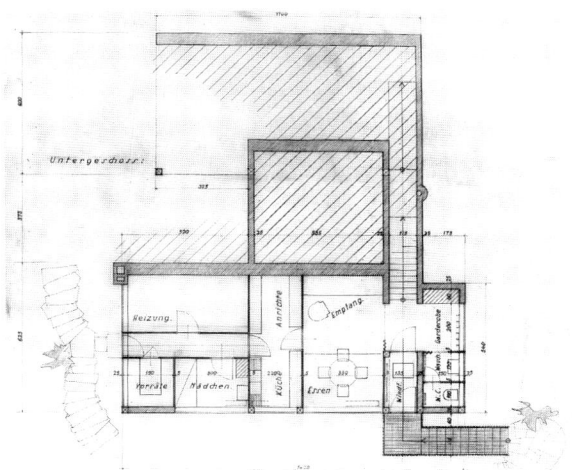

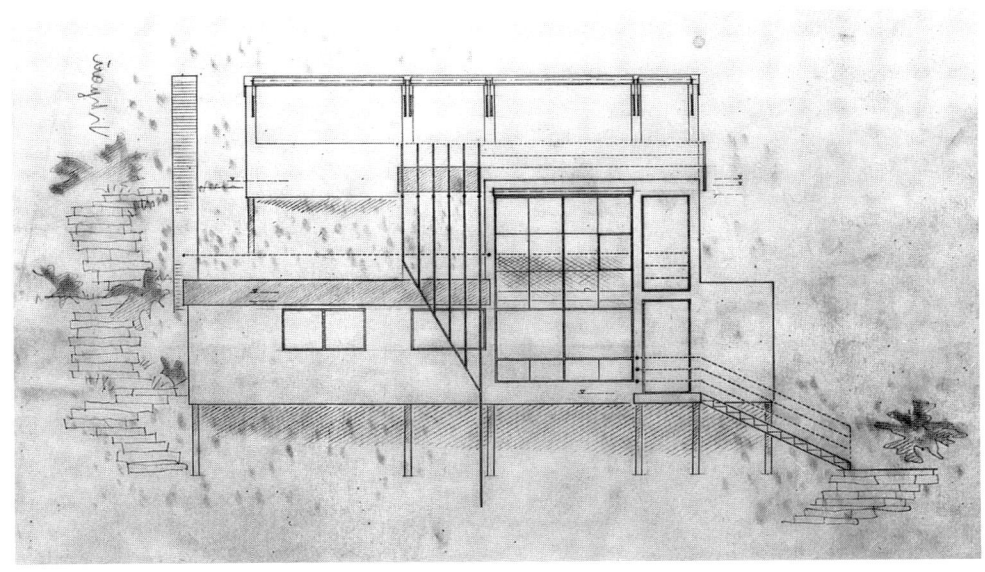

1935 House for Dr Baensch, Berlin-Spandau

The house for the jurist Felix Baensch is a most impressive illustration of the principle of organic spatial movement evolved by Scharoun between 1934 and 1945. Here, Scharoun managed to adapt to the traditional materials and construction methods demanded by the Third Reich while continuing to develop his interests in an articulated plan, improved spatial qualities and applications of building elements.

Only the street elevation and individual lines of the plan still appear to start from an ordering geometry: on the garden side, the spaces and walls are fully dissolved, as is vividly shown by the wall next to the terrace door, with its seemingly unfinished, random brick structure. The internal spatial relationships are determined by a diagonal axis arising from the opening out of the rooms, the orientation of views towards Lake Havel and the use of the dining room as a spatial divider. Following the slope of the site, the house is set on three different levels which form spoke-like terraces, funnelling down into the round dining room. The patterns of use and orientation of the rooms are precisely determined by paths of movement and function: the studio is placed in the west, where it is protected from direct sunlight; the concert grand piano is set to one side of the circulation, in a special place of its own; the round form of the dining room, which is directly connected to the kitchen and the hall, responds to the round dining table. The arrangement of the upper storey, however, is quite different to the ground level; its rooms also occasionally have arbitrary acute and obtuse corners.

South elevation.

Ground-floor plan.

The stepped living room with view of the Havel.

Living room with piano and window.

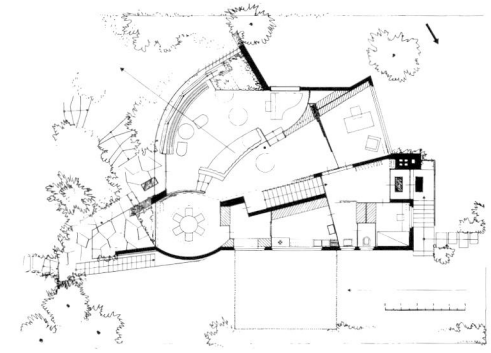

1936/37   Oskar Moll House, Berlin-Grunewald

The studio house in Berlin-Grunewald, next to Lake Halen, was built for Oskar Moll, the painter and Head of the Breslau Academy of Arts, where Scharoun taught. In this project the rooms are interlocked both horizontally and vertically in a considered way. The living spaces are orientated towards the lake, as in the Baensch House. The main floor is split over three different levels. In the centre are the dining room and stairs, which serve to divide the space. On the north side is the artist's studio with a large north window at its highest point. This room also has views towards the south over the garden and the lake.

In a lecture on 23 June 1952, Scharoun emphasized the organic-functional nature of the non-orthogonal corners in the house: 'the Moll House was based not on a geometric principle but on a system of interconnections – in contrast to the many-roomed "villa" in which the living spaces fulfil technical and economic requirements but are subordinate to financial and geometrical constraints. I will show you, using the example of the Moll House, that giving up the right angle and the free form is not an act of wilfulness, but a true response to the landscape and the needs of the people.'

Southwest elevation, plan and sections.

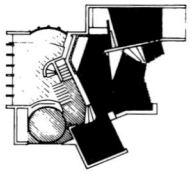

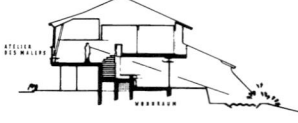

Artist's studio.

Living room.

1937 Ferdinand Möller House, Zermützelsee near Altruppin, Brandenburg

In 1932, Scharoun worked on several projects for a house in Potsdam for Ferdinand Möller. These early designs were still wholly in a rectilinear style. The original intention at Zermützelsee was to build a large single-family home: a change of fortunes, however, meant that only a summer house was built (see Introduction).

The Möller House retains elements of previous designs: the orthogonally defined functional rooms, the free dissolution of living spaces towards the garden, the movement along a diagonal axis which determined the plan. The changing character of the plan is particularly evident in this phase of Scharoun's work: though the plan here is still basically orthogonal, it is undergoing a process of dissolution. In 1952 Scharoun said that this house was fully in the spirit of Martin Heidegger and Hugo Häring, responding to the conditions of nature and the essential character of the dwelling: 'The functions were set out and after an initial investigation of them and their relationship to the surrounding environment I prepared a preliminary design, arranging the space in such a way that the sense of place resulted from the structure, from the relationships of the places to each other and their surroundings.

'Next these "places" were marked out, tried out, on the building site, to determine their position and height relative to each other and their surroundings. The house then became, in the terms of Hugo Häring, a form for living in, a "shell" for the processes of living, and thus the form arose in the manner of the organic work.'

Southwest elevation.

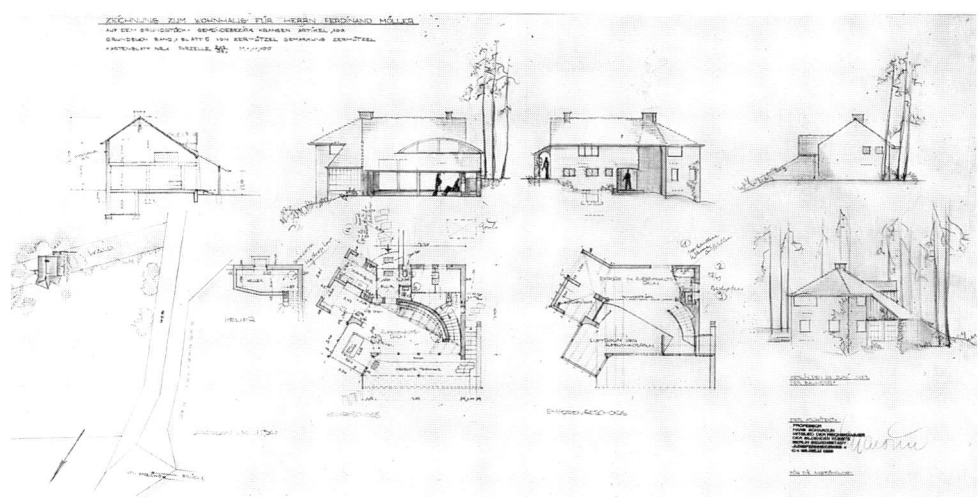

Elevations and plans.

Living room with gallery.

1946 Berlin plans – a first report
Plan for the reconstruction of Berlin, exhibition in the White Hall of Berlin Castle
Scharoun, with a planning collective comprised of Wils Ebert, Peter Friedrich, Ludmilla Herzenstein, Reinhold Lingner, Louise Seitz, Seman Selmanagic

Scharoun was made Head of the Greater Berlin Department of Housing and Building on 17 May 1945, soon after the surrender of the Third Reich. Shortly after his appointment, he formed a collective which produced a plan for the reconstruction of Greater Berlin, unsanctioned by the Allies. The group's main intention was to counter the general feeling of uncertainty with a plan conceived from the German standpoint, to make a political gesture by saying that there had to be a clear principle behind the planning of Greater Berlin: that it was not enough to just clear away the rubble. The collective included a number of architects who had been active participants in the pre-war CIAM Congresses, most notably Wils Ebert and Selman Selmanagic.

The group wanted to create an 'urban landscape' that reflected the spirit and structure of the medieval city, but not its appearance. It believed that the historical concentric development of Berlin had impeded effective traffic planning and land use, and therefore proposed an alternative – a series of parallel 'residential and commercial areas, each developed around its own core'. The residential areas were to be concentrated in well-defined 'neighbourhoods', small enough to be crossed on foot in ten to fifteen minutes. These neighbourhoods would contain school buildings, cultural facilities and, where possible, places of work, to minimize the need for road travel. Major road axes both linked the different neighbourhoods and acted as boundaries between them: to avoid traffic congestion, the roads ran parallel to each other, and not towards a common centre. The layout of the road network and residential areas followed the east-west axis of the Spree Valley. Where possible the plan made use of existing streets, but extended them to form an orthogonal traffic grid.

The 'collective plan' was presented to the public in 1946 in an exhibition, 'Berlin plans – a first report', in the White Hall of the (then still intact) Berlin Castle. The plan was admittedly utopian and primarily intended to provoke further discussion – in fact, it unleashed wide-

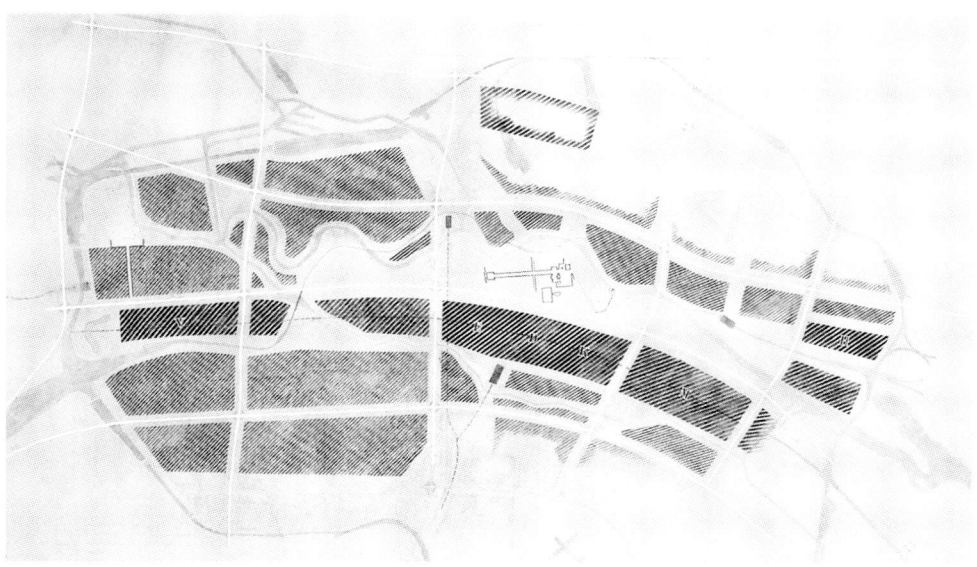

'Collective plan'.

spread criticism, on account of its schematic division of residential and working areas, supply networks and traffic systems. Though the plan made a deliberate, radical departure from the past by doing away with the axial planning of Martin Mächler and Albert Speer, it also destroyed the concentric ring system within the city. Most commonly, people complained that the plan failed to address immediate problems such as clearing the rubble and providing housing. Many also objected to its underlying philosophy.

1948   Exhibition pavilion for the Gerd Rosen Gallery, Berlin
Project

This pavilion for the book- and art-dealer Gerd Rosen was one of Scharoun's first projects after the war. It is a hybrid work – the design process continues to be centred around the plan, while the form returns to the Modern vocabulary that Scharoun used before 1933. The focal point is a staircase which serves not only to divide the pavilion but also to organize spatially the different levels of exhibition elements. Here too Scharoun used diagonals derived from the path of movement to break up and enliven an orthogonal form. The diagonals terminate in a small sculpture garden on one side and an oblique-angled ramp on the other.

Plan, section and elevation.

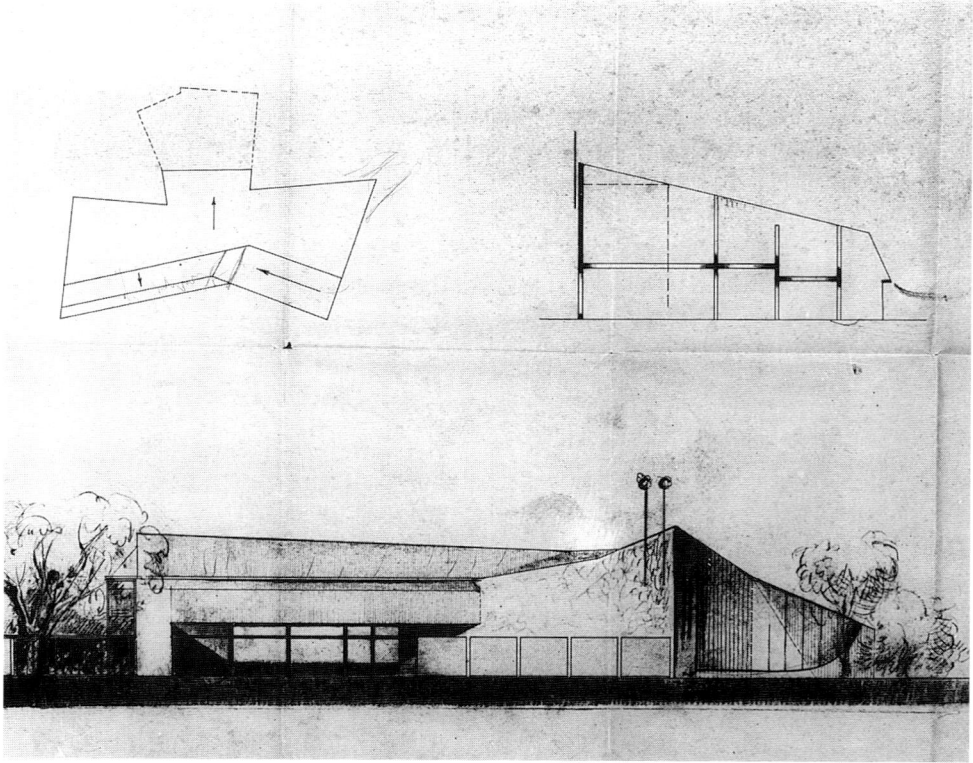

Ground-floor plan.

Model.

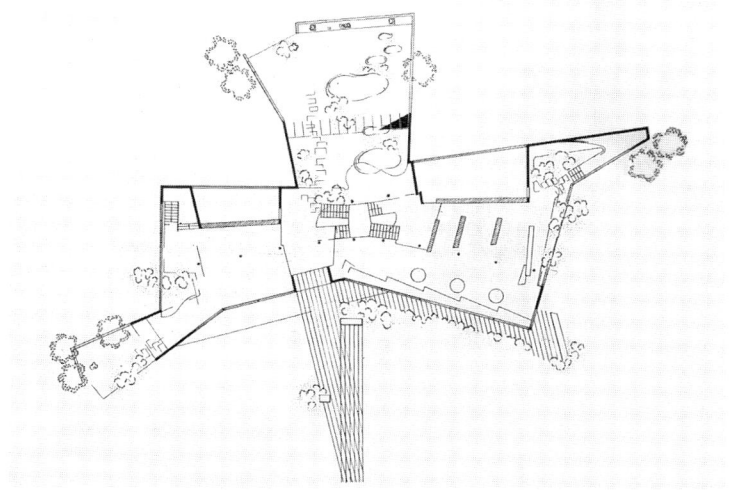

1949 Stuttgart Music Hall
Competition design, first prize

The Music Hall in Stuttgart was one of Scharoun's first 'projects for the community' after the war. It generated fundamental spatial arrangements that he would develop further in later designs for concert halls and theatres.

Scharoun's explanatory text states: '... The whole complex – though accentuated by large spaces – is interspersed with numerous smaller spaces, which serve everyday functions and ensure a constant flow of activity.

'It seems important to avoid any sense of "dead space". Accordingly, the large spaces are always light and well lit, not waiting for the night to come to life. To achieve this, there is a skylit roof above which a supporting superstructure carries sun-control screens. The whole complex becomes optically transparent; the space can be divided up by curtains or other means.

'The siting responds to the natural conditions of the landscape and both existing and future development. The hall breaks away from the narrow, gently sloping confines of the city and opens up to the breadth, the light and the profiles of the mountains surrounding the valley basin.

'The terrace-restaurant on the fly-tower also plays an important role in establishing a link with the landscape. This element not only forms a counterpoint to the existing and planned large buildings around the intersection of the Schloß- and Seidenstraße, but also accentuates the border between the Kriegsberg and the valley in which the Music Hall and the proposed lakeside complex lie. The aim of the planning was to achieve an intensive link with the natural features that are part of Stuttgart's charm. The rooms are adaptable and light and can be animated at any time, accommodating life on both an intimate and a monumental scale...'

Elevations.

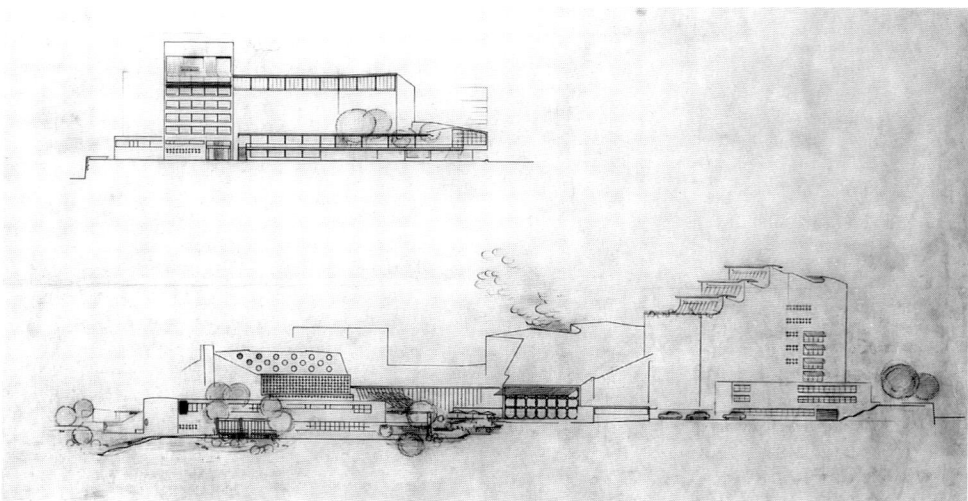

Concert hall, perspective.

Plan at base level.

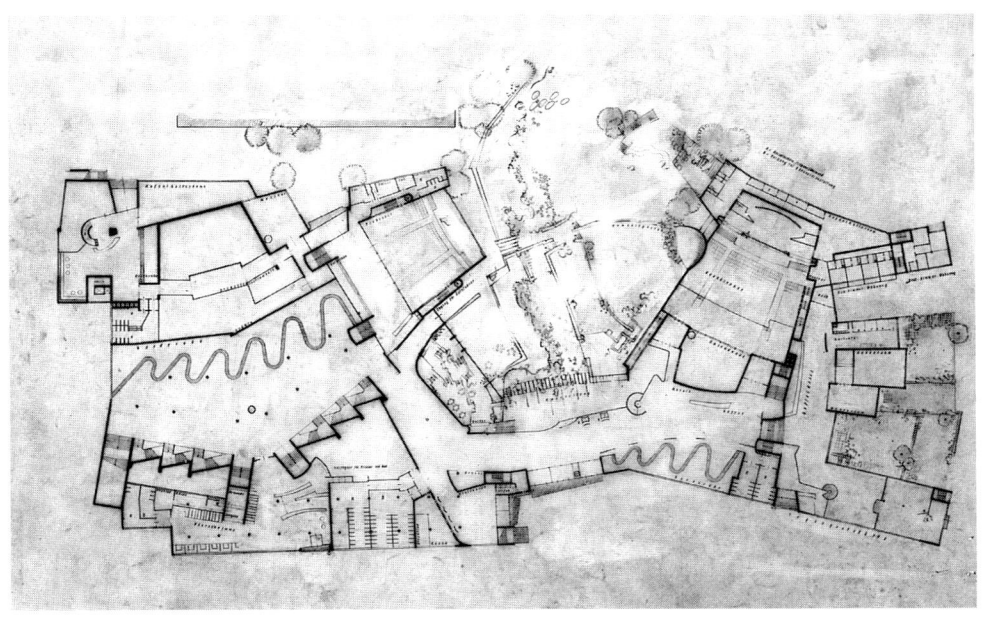

1950 Schminke House, Celle
Project

This small house was planned to replace Scharoun's first house for the Schminke family in Löbau, Saxony, which became Polish territory after the war. The motto of the project was 'living on the sunny side': the obtuse-angled, elongated living spaces are orientated towards the sun, as in Scharoun's early single-family houses, while the orthogonal functional rooms are placed behind them, to the north. The contours of the site are followed by a curve that runs between the entrance and the kitchen, dividing the building in two on the north side. Since the house was not intended for a large family, there is no determining subdivision of spaces: the entrance is placed to the north, next to the bedroom. It leads directly into the dining room, which connects through to the kitchen and bathroom and the living area. The living area is divided into three distinct sections. The narrow sitting room leads to the hearth, then to a special space for the grand piano in the west. The rather awkward location of the bathroom reflects the fact that Scharoun had limited space and money for the service areas and concentrated instead on creating useful, spatially differentiated living areas.

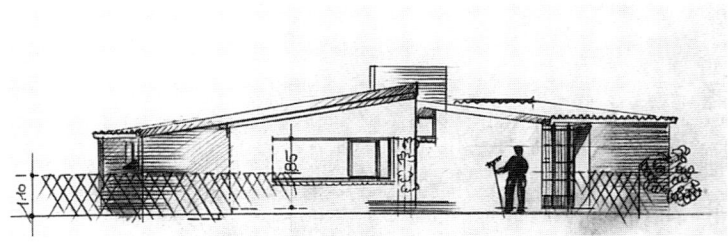

Elevation.

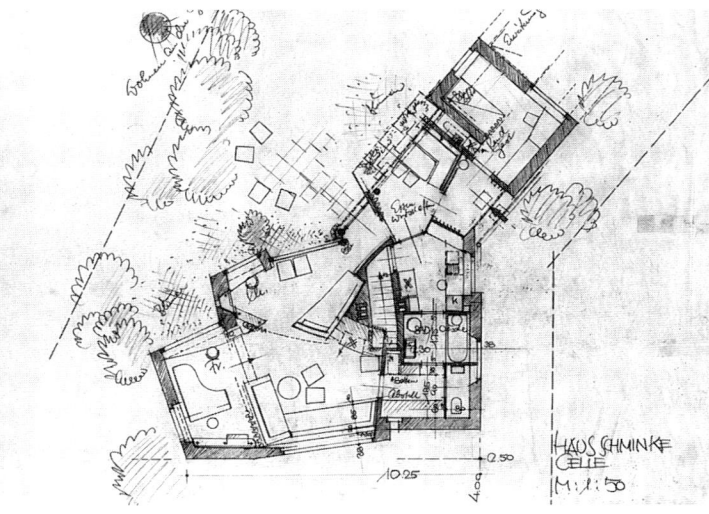

Plan.

1951   Elementary school, Darmstadt
Project

In 1951 the city of Darmstadt commissioned eleven major public buildings, including schools, cultural facilities and a hospital, as part of an initiative called 'People and Space'. Scharoun produced a design which as a prototype contributed to the debate in the 1950s on the design of schools and brought him subsequent similar commissions in Lünen (1956) and Marl (1960). The design is determined not just by functional requirements, but by the results of an intensive investigation of the social role of the school and the needs of the pupils. In the explanatory text and later publications, Scharoun referred to the universality of the basic principles developed in the Darmstadt school. He saw the school as a reflection, in microcosm, of the city. The building is not formally closed, but consists of many functional units which relate to one another in a variety of ways. The classrooms are in three separate units, each containing three years of the school. Equipped with their own common rooms and cloakrooms, these units form enclosed small communities – 'secret areas', in Scharoun's words – within the school community as a whole. The siting of the building and the choice of colours inside depends on the age of the pupils. The school house for classes 1 to 3 is orientated towards the south: the youngest pupils, who are making the transition from parental home to schoool, still need to feel the 'warmth of the nest' – hence the direct sunlight and the strong colours. The rooms are intended to accommodate the children's behaviour as a group and their desire for movement, so the 'form of the room has an educational, a social and a health aspect'. The second area is for classes 4 to 6. These are placed east to west, to express the different nature of these years of learning, which Scharoun characterized as 'recognizing, understanding and experiencing interests in lessons and independent activities'. In the last group, classes 7 to 9, the predominant issues are the development of the 'self' and the community. At this age, children are defining their personality, turning their investigations and studies inwards, representing themselves, informing themselves. Accordingly, the classrooms are orientated to the north and have excellent indirect natural light.

The centre of the school is an interconnecting artery, a 'path for meeting' with additional facilities such as the assembly hall, staffrooms, gymnasium and work rooms. The assembly hall forms what Scharoun called a 'mediating room' – an 'open area' for pupils to mix, not only with their classmates but also with pupils from other schools in the city. The 'semi-open area' – the fields for games, sports and athletics – lies at the other end of the school. Between the individual areas are the religion and biology classrooms and a place for noticeboards. At the eastern end of the school is the 'Cosmic Room' which represents man's relationship to the cosmos in spatial form. Here we see a microcosmic representation of a world-view that would be expressed later in the 'landscape' of the Philharmonie and 'roofscape' of the State Library. The dome of the Cosmic Room symbolizes the heavens; the floor contains a concentric square and circle, symbolizing both the earth, in the platonic sense, and the cosmos. The passage of the seasons and the sun are represented in a similar manner. The building is largely glazed, allowing people outside to look in and experience the 'inner order'.

In his project for the Darmstadt school, Scharoun tackled issues of a complexity rare at the time. He described basic principles underlying the design:

1. The expression of a universal democratic principle. The position of the individual *vis-à-vis* the community and the school community is made clear in the structure of the school, which emphasizes the responsibility of the individual and an awareness of the democratic principle.

2. Teaching methods must take account of the progressive development of the child's spiritual and physical powers. This factor, combined with the desire to create specific teaching environments, gives rise to a type of school which adapts to changing pedagogical needs – which in turn should have an effect on the form of the school community.

3. The incorporation of the factor of time. Scharoun intended the design of the Darmstadt school to clearly represent the fourth dimension: '... the new physical representation of time that we see in the paintings of both Picasso and, in my opinion, Braque, can perhaps also be expressed in a building through an attempt to make the different stages of consciousness, their clear polar relationships, the fundamental basis of the plan.'

Model and proposed plan. Right-hand page: perspective.

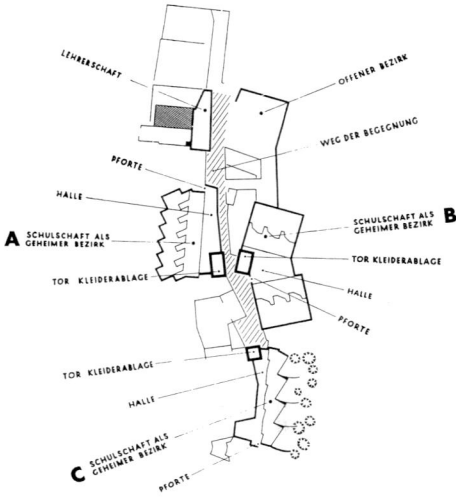

1952   Heinrich Mendelsohn high-rise, Berlin-Charlottenburg
Competition entry, with Sergius Ruegenberg and Chen Kuan Lee

In 1951 the developer Heinrich Mendelsohn sponsored an ideas competition for a commercial building between the Kaiserdamm and Lietzensee in Berlin, which attracted 133 entries.
The brief required the narrow point of the triangular site to be left free, in order to create a stronger link between the park and the Kaiserdamm. The building itself had to be an imposing solitary form. Scharoun's project is ordered according to functionally derived spatial inter-relationships. It emphasizes the corner situation, as the counterpoint to nearby structures. The sail-like roof profiles and the asymmetrical building elements make a formal reference to projects that Scharoun designed during the war and depicted in watercolours. They are also quintessentially of the 1950s. The design did not win a prize as the jury, which included both Hans and Wassili Luckhardt, preferred clearer forms like a rectangular solid or a three-spoked high-rise.

Bird's eye view.

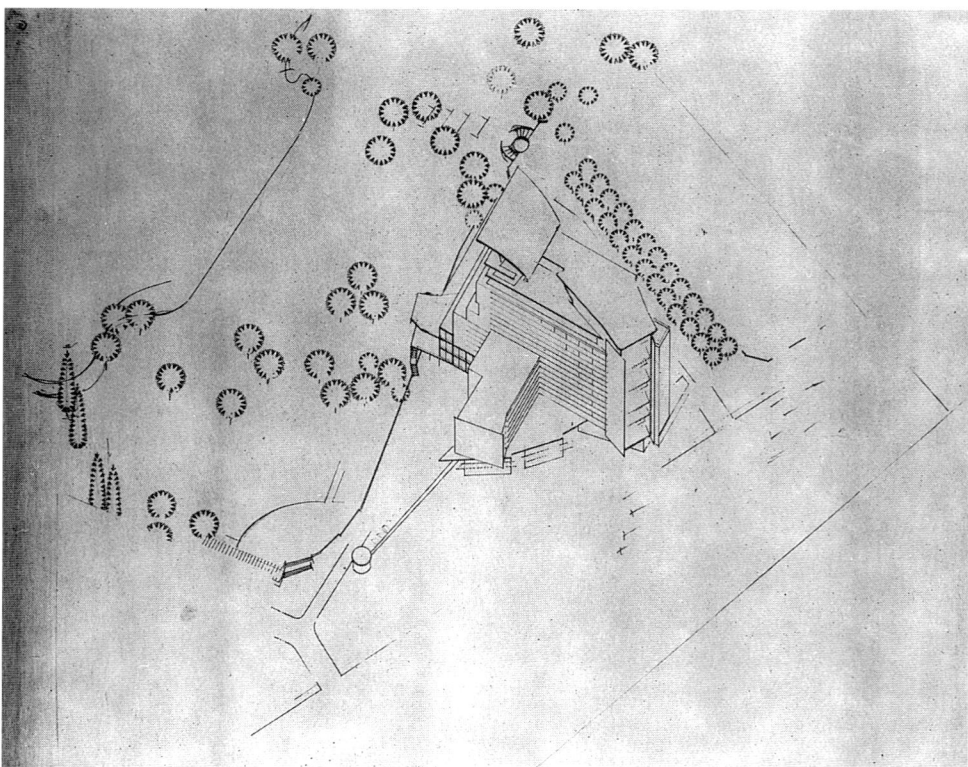

1952–1954   Kassel State Theatre
Competition entry and developed design, with Hermann Mattern and Willem Huller

When Scharoun won first prize in the Kassel Theatre competition it seemed he would at last have the opportunity to apply the principles of organic architecture to a large project. The new building was to replace a theatre at the end of the Friedrichplatz that had been largely destroyed during the war.

Scharoun set his design slightly off the axis of the Friedrichplatz in order to open up views of the landscape. A pedestrian bridge links the theatre with the square. A sense of closure is achieved with a fly-tower whose asymmetrical curving form embraces the spaces in front, rather than tower up above them. The front of house – consisting of the auditorium, foyer and entrance area – is not tied together formally, but arranged as a series of distinct spaces which terrace down to the square. The fly-tower skilfully links the side stages, technical and ancillary spaces. To the right of the main stage, within the remaining walls of the original theatre, there is a studio theatre linked to the scene stores via the side stage of the main theatre.

The shape of the main theatre is determined by the broad open stage which Scharoun developed in collaboration with the set designer Willem Huller. The proscenium arch is low, in order to 'make use of the latest developments in lighting technology'. To either side of this horizon are vertical housings for services and spotlights for 'profile-inducing side-lighting' or 'silhouetting back-lighting'.

In front of the auditorium was a series of differentiated spaces – foyer, cloakrooms, a garden courtyard and a snack bar – which opened like windbreaks, setting curved elements against each other. Visitors to the theatre would have experienced a series of constantly changing and colliding spaces – a sensation Scharoun later recreated in the foyers of the Philharmonie and the Wolfsburg Theatre. Though the space appears irrational, it is in fact clearly ordered. The visitor enters the foyer and ticket office either from the main approach or from the pedestrian bridge above. To the right are cloakrooms for that side of the auditorium; beyond the cloakrooms are stairs which lead down to the stalls and up to the circle. A further passage from the foyer leads directly to the stalls and the lobby on the right-hand side of the lower level. A result of this complex horizontal arrangement is the breaking up of the vertical organization linking foyer to auditorium.

The foyer area is set over five different levels, separated by short flights of stairs. The slope of the auditorium takes up the natural slope of the site. The new theatre, like its predecessor, is set into the hillside, preventing the building mass as a whole from appearing too high. The mass of the theatre is also reduced by the external stepping of the elements of the building, which directly reflects the interlocking of the different levels inside.

The competition entry accentuates the amorphous forms of the cloakrooms, which play on the oval form of the main stage. However, in the working drawings of 1953/54, the formal vocabulary is rationalized: the rounded, curved lines give way to straight lines, which collide at acute or obtuse angles – and the oval form of the cloakrooms disappears altogether.

The competition model indicates an architectural separation between the stage and the administrative offices on one hand, and the auditorium and foyer on the other. The first area is rational and orthogonally ordered, whilst the second area contains curved walls that flow into each other. In the reworked design the fly-tower and administrative area are pulled together and placed across the mass of the building as its tallest part. In this phase, Scharoun formulated the idea of the 'building crown' which would become the dominant feature of later works – the Mannheim Theatre project, the Philharmonie, State Library and Wolfsburg Theatre. The linked but disparate forms of the competion entry give way, in the revised design, to a more homogenous overall appearance, altogether more angled and skewed, with fewer soft forms – a step towards the crystalline style which became explicit in Scharoun's late work, particularly the Wolfsburg Theatre.

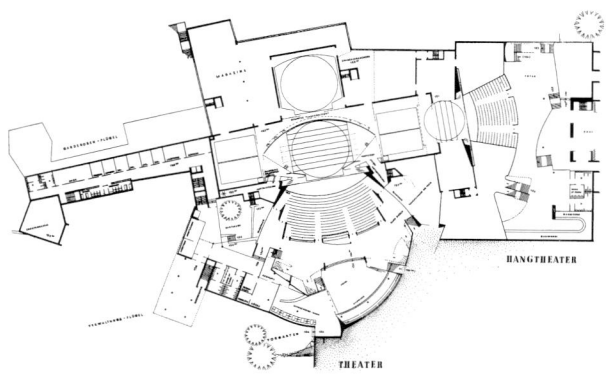

Competition entry, ground plan.

Competition model.

Model of final building.

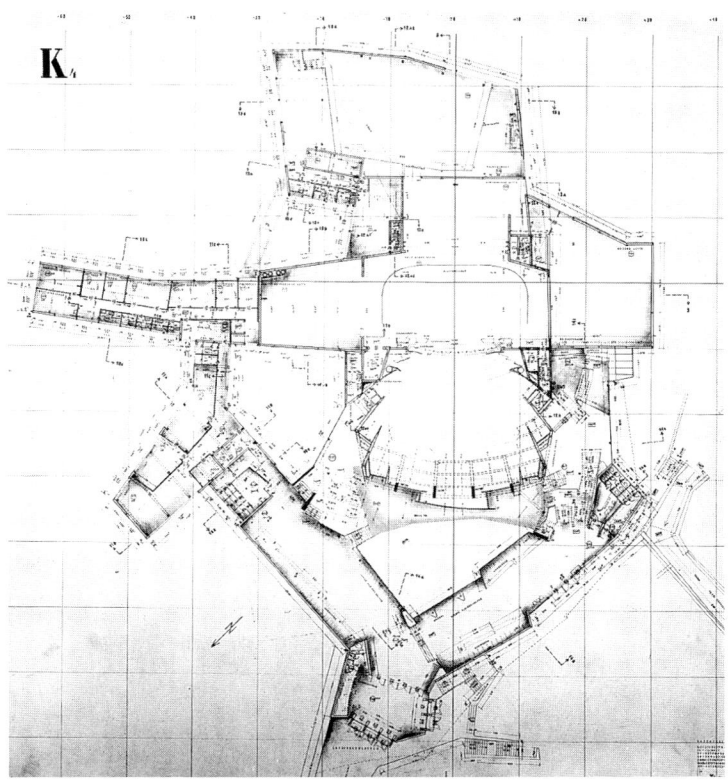

Plan as built.

1953 Mannheim National Theatre
Competition design

In the National Theatre in Mannheim Scharoun developed a model for the asymmetrical theatre. Scharoun set his project in the Goetheplatz, which was the site of the final building. The old town of Mannheim has an orthogonal grid iron of streets running mainly north, south, east and west. Scharoun attempted to subvert this grid with the mass of the building without altering the rectangular Goetheplatz. His idea, which was simple but effective, was to place the building diagonally in the square, taking advantage of a similarly oblique main street. The primary building mass, which brought together the stage and administrative area, stands on the diagonal, while the masses of the small and large auditoriums, positioned at each corner, stand at an angle to the rest of the building. The outer form of the building also indicates the main theme of the interior: asymmetry. The main stage has a 27-metre opening and shallow proportions to emphasize the progression of scenes characteristic of the a-perspective theatre. The stalls are divided into three sections and set slightly off axis, at an angle to the stage.

In his project description, Scharoun referred repeatedly to the multi-functional nature of the stage – a major requirement for theatres at the time – although it contradicted his concept of a stage designed for specific plays.

Daylight could be brought into both theatres: in the main theatre, it could even be controlled by a mechanically operated opening in the roof.

Diagram of the variants.

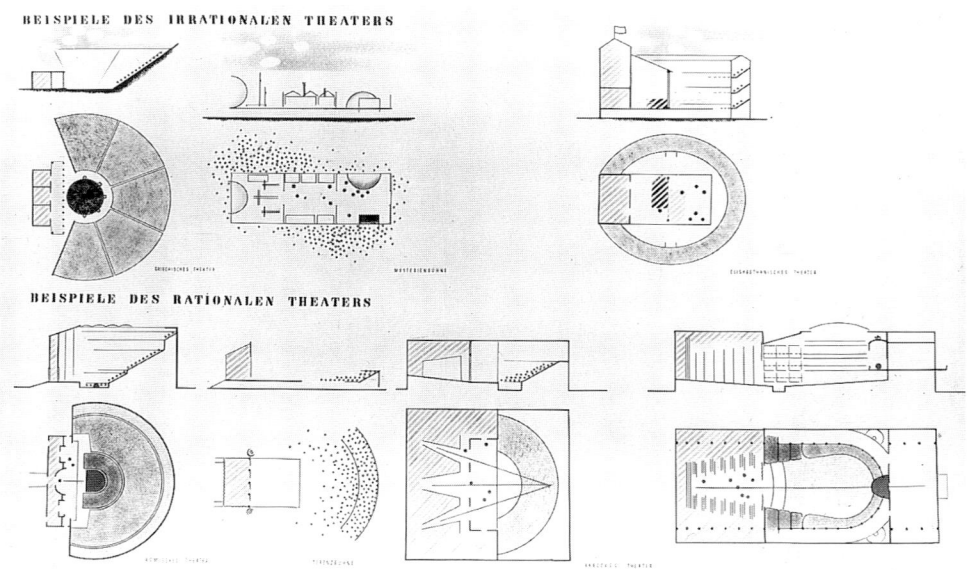

A fixed fee of DM 8000 was allocated for a second limited competition between the practices of Mies van der Rohe (Chicago), Scharoun (Berlin), Schwarz/Riphahn/Bernhard (Cologne), Döcker (Stuttgart), Schweizer (Karlsruhe), Perrottet/Stoecklin/Baur (Basle), Lange/Mitzlaff (Mannheim), Schmechel/Thoma (Mannheim), Marx/Wagner/Au (Mannheim) and Plattner/Mündel (Mannheim). In September 1953 Mies van der Rohe, Schwarz and Schweizer were asked to develop their designs, but ultimately the commission went to Gerhard Weber.

Plan and model.

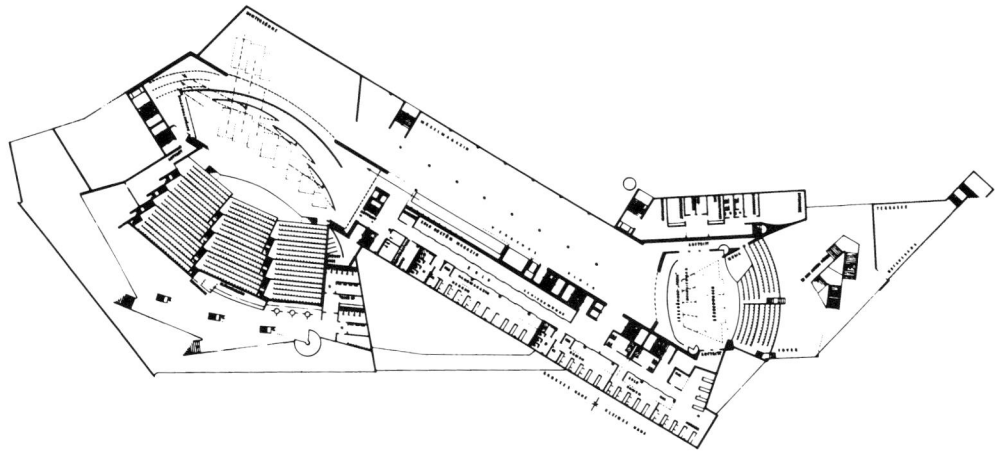

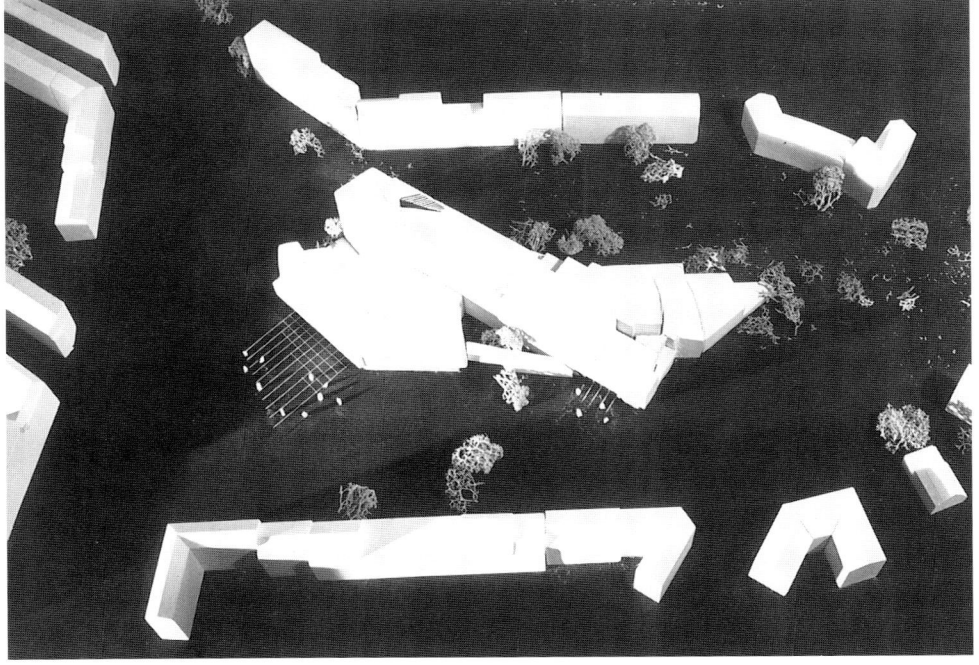

1954–1959   'Romeo and Juliet' high-rises, Stuttgart-Zuffenhausen
With Wilhelm Frank

The Romeo and Juliet high-rises were Scharoun's first built works after the war, after years of participating in numerous competitions. They can be seen as the prototypes for subsequent larger housing projects, mainly in Berlin and the Stuttgart area.

The names for the two high-rises were inspired by their different masses. The Juliet building is stepped on the fourth, seventh and eleventh floors and contains 82 apartments arranged in a circle and opening up to a central area via pergolas. The 19-storey Romeo building has six apartments on each floor (104 in all) which are entered through an internal corridor. Romeo contains one- to four-bedroom apartments of between 38 and 96 square metres; Juliet has three- and four-bedroom units of between 72 and 86 square metres. The façades are jagged, with projecting balconies. Columns of individual apartments are defined by the vertical breaks of the staircases and lift shafts. The apartments have unusual, non-orthogonal plans. They open up in a fan shape, with the living spaces on the outside and the utility rooms on the inside. In the Juliet building light and air are brought to the inner area by the pergolas. Unusually for the time, all the apartments were privately owned – a major factor in ensuring their economic success. The project led to subsequent commissions for the 'Salute' high-rise in Stuttgart and the 'Orplid' apartment house and 'Rauhe Kapf' *Siedlung* in Böblingen. Significantly, Scharoun managed to give the high-rises a positive identity in a relatively featureless location. The façades and plans of Romeo and Juliet remain an almost paradigmatic illustration of the contrast between the organic solution and the orthogonal, cubic or rectangular high-rise.

Bird's eye view of 'Romeo and Juliet'.

View of 'Juliet'.

Typical plans of 'Romeo' (left) and 'Juliet' (right).

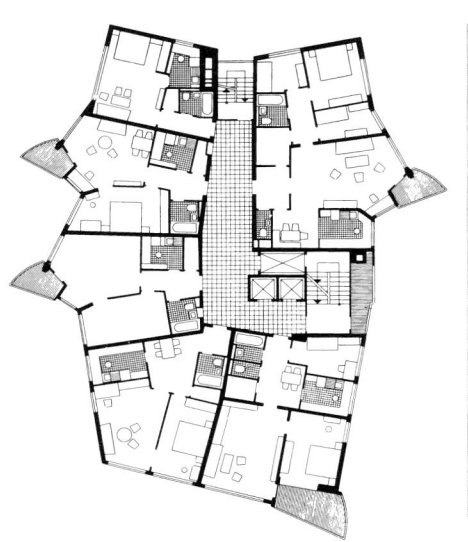

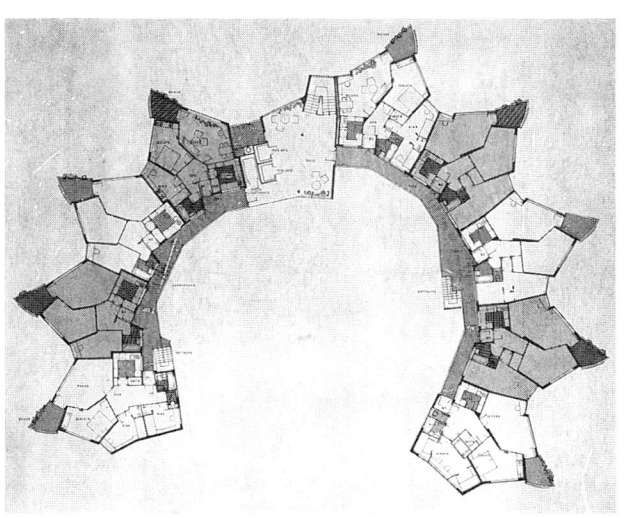

1956–1961 Charlottenburg-Nord *Siedlung*, Berlin

In 1955 the non-profit housing association GSW commissioned Scharoun, in his capacity as Head of the Institute for Urban Development at the Technische Universität in Berlin, to undertake a basic urban-planning study of the area between Wedding and Spandau, which encompassed the Siemensstadt *Siedlung* he had planned in 1930. The plan adopted the idea of the 'ribbon city' proposed in the 1946 collective plan for Berlin, but on a smaller scale. It also studied the implications of demographic change on the planning of individual dwellings and the development as a whole. The built result of the study was – despite some changes and much trimming of costs – Scharoun's largest housing project, the Charlottenburg-Nord *Siedlung*.

The *Siedlung* is characterized externally by 'settlements' which curve in towards each other, evoking the 'horseshoe' forms of Bruno Taut's and Martin Wagner's Hufeisensiedlung. This gave rise to a wide variety of ground-plans, with as many as 36 different types in a single 'settlement'.

The explanatory text written by the architect and the GSW states: 'The landscape of the planning area is determined in essence by the east-west orientation of the Spree Valley. The existing forms of development and land ownership run parallel to this, forming connected bands of related use: 1. industrial and light-industrial areas, 2. housing (existing housing developments), 3. open spaces (Jungfernheide and Spree Valley).

These conditions determine the linear nature of the proposed development, which also encompasses the land to the east of the Hinkeldeydamm ... The principle behind the traffic planning applies not just to the development area but to the city as a whole. There must be an overall structuring order, in which the traffic routes are separated according to function ...

'Berlin has an increasing network of expressways which divide the residential and the commercial districts into distinct areas varying in size from 10 to 25 square kilometres – A recognition of the importance of the proposed development area in relation to the city as a whole, both in housing and commercial terms, led us to undertake thorough research, using all available data, to clarify the demographic and sociological structures of individual families and the social community as a whole. This picture has been markedly affected by post-war change, with obvious implications for future developments. Demographic forecasts point clearly to a trend towards smaller families. This affects the size of housing required both today and in the future. It is not sufficient, however, to analyse housing needs solely according to the number of people in families; sociological structures must also be taken into account. We studied occupations and household structures and defined a median area which encompasses the great majority of types ... Our investigations suggest that in the case of Berlin the number of occupants in a housing block should be raised from 450 to around 650, and that two such blocks with around 1300 inhabitants would be able to support certain social and cultural facilities. From the form of the block we were able to make important deductions about the form of the individual "settlements" and how they should relate to each other. Their development must be clarified further. New forms must undoubtedly be evolved to give visual expression to this character of symbiosis.

'It appeared important to establish a clear relationship between the primary and secondary schools and the open spaces. The siting of the schools links them with the path leading to the green space (north of the residential zone), which is intended primarily for pedestrians and cyclists.

'As new industrial facilities are to be built in Siemensstadt, we propose also to provide low- and high-rise "worker's housing" ... in areas with good traffic connections, within the industrial areas themselves, and on the outskirts of existing residential neighbourhoods.'

Overall site plan of *Siedlung* (left) and plan of apartment.

View of a row of housing.

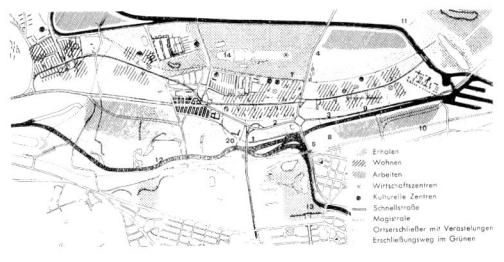

1956   Development plan for the Hansa district, Berlin-Tiergarten
Project

The Hansa district was the first large-scale project in the reconstruction of the inner city of Berlin. It grew out of the idea of organizing an International Building Exhibition (Interbau Berlin 1957), similar in spirit to the Weissenhof Exhibition, to demonstrate guidelines for public building in the future. The widespread destruction had created what the planners called a 'fresh-start situation'. A committee was formed under the chairmanship of Otto Bartning to select participating architects and coordinate the work. Ultimately the project involved 54 architects from 13 countries. Most of the older architects belonged to the CIAM or Ring Group.

The starting-point for the project was a competition-winning development plan by Willy Kreuer and Gerhard Jobst, which the jury described as 'attractively differentiated without being schematic'. The plan adopts the model of the 'dispersed' city, but without the grid-arranged housing blocks that were typical of CIAM. Spaces are roughly outlined and even the historic Hansaplatz is surrounded by housing blocks. The ordering principles, however, are at too large a scale to be perceived within the city itself.

At one meeting of the committee, J. B. Bakema urged that the development plan should shift from a high-density arrangement which followed the circulation pattern to an orthogonal order which emphasized the independence of the individual building elements. This was a decisive alteration of Kreuer and Jobst's competition scheme. It gave a more concise formal expression to an apparently arbitrary plan. Patterns and landmarks were taken into account: the historical axis of the Altonaer Straße towards the Victory Column, for example, was emphasized by a funnelling of the housing blocks. Individual areas also appeared to be more sharply accentuated, as demonstrated by the enclosing of the Hansaplatz with new buildings – although this could only be seen from the air.

The Ring Group around Scharoun put forward their own version of the plan which gave even stronger emphasis to the notion of the square, proposing concentrically ordered housing which made reference to the radial form of the previous housing on the site. This plan also distinguished between high-rise constructions in the centre and lower, denser buildings in the surrounding area.

The scheme as built represented a compromise between all of these thoughts. The dominant element was Bakema's orthogonal ordering, but the Ring project ensured that some low buildings were built in addition to the high-rises.

Model of the circular scheme around Scharoun.

1956 Single-family houses for the Hansa district, Berlin-Tiergarten
Project

The Interbau Exhibition involved a large number of the well-known architects of the time. Its catalogue indicates that Scharoun was supposed to build five single-family homes in the Hansa district – though the project never went ahead as the site was allocated to the Academy of Arts. Scharoun's first proposal shows five houses; his second three, all with articulated ground-plans which seem directly related to the projects he designed between 1933 and 1937. The one-and-a-half-storey houses are orientated south, towards the adjacent English Garden. They were intended to illustrate new possibilities for larger social housing. The focal point is the living area, with a conservatory to the east and access, via stairs, to the roof terrace to the west. Grouped in a wide semicircle around the living area are the kitchen and utility rooms (to the east) and the entrance and bedrooms (to the southwest). The varying slopes of the tent-like roof admit top light from various directions, amplifying the natural light in individual rooms and tying them more directly to the surrounding landscape and the climate.

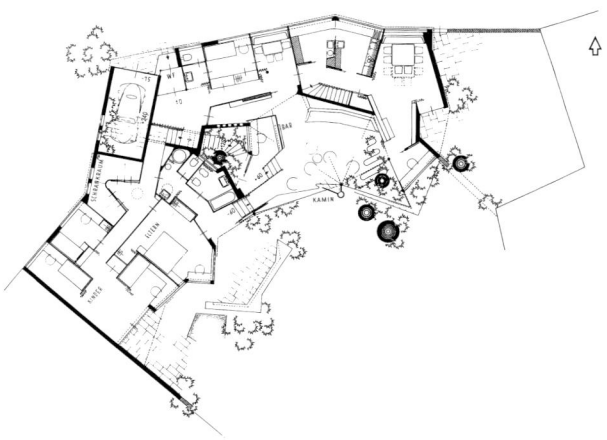

Plan.

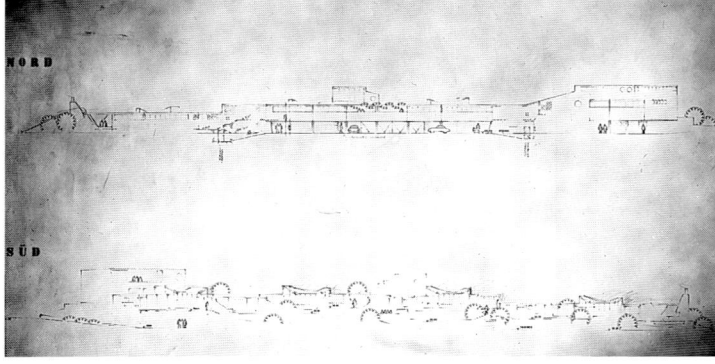

Elevations.

1956–1963 Concert Hall for the Berlin Philharmonic Orchestra, Bundesallee, Berlin-Wilmersdorf, and Kemperplatz, Berlin-Tiergarten
Competition entry, first prize

In mid-1956 twelve architects were invited to participate in a limited competition for a new building to house the Berlin Philharmonic Orchestra. Scharoun won, supported from early on by Herbert von Karajan, who wrote in a letter to the jury: 'Of all the entries, our overwhelming preference is for the one which essentially strives to incorporate the mass from which sound emerges into the middle of the hall (the number of the model escapes me, but it is white, with a gold base) – I know of no existing concert hall which resolves the seating problem in such an ideal way as this design. The positioning of the orchestra practically in the middle of the space also seems to – allow a hitherto unparalleled opportunity to experiment and to express the Philharmonic Orchestra's typical style of musical interpretation, which is characterized by a long, expansive projection and a particular pause at the beginning and end of a musical sequence. We have a few small reservations – but these are trivial in comparison to the quality of the project as a whole, which I cannot recommend warmly enough.'

Scharoun himself wrote on 2 September 1957 in an article entitled 'Music in the Middle –':
'The most immediate consideration was this: is it mere chance that, whenever people hear improvised music, they immediately gather round in a circle? I set myself the task of translating to the concert hall this quite natural process, whose psychological aspect everyone can understand. The music should also provide the spatial and visual focus. This was the starting-point for the form of the Philharmonie. But the design was made spatially and technically feasible only by advances in acoustic science. "New territory" was conquered and developed here in close collaboration with the acoustic engineer, Professor Cremer.

'Although the orchestra is not exactly in the centre of the space, it is surrounded by the public as in an amphitheatre. This arrangement of the space, which contains seating for 2220, means that the distance between members of the audience is relatively small. Also, there is no circle. For both these reasons, there is little need to direct sound at the public.

'The articulated space gives a lively structure to the body of the audience, allowing the dynamic movements of the orchestra and conductor to be observed from a variety of aspects. The audience is tied to the action, rather than viewing it as a separate event on the stage.

'The "atmosphere" of a concert hall is naturally important. In this respect, light has a special role to play in the new Philharmonie. Today's lighting technology is excellent for setting a scene, lending support to the design of the hall. It is intended to also use the 'acoustic backdrop' as a vehicle of lighting – making it possible to light the orchestra in an unobtrusive way. Further sources of light are distributed over the walls and roof.

'The architectural treatment aims to give the hall a certain intimacy, countering the monumentality of the building as a whole. Intimacy is essential for direct engagement in the musical event, for individual, creative participation...'

From the outset, there were doubts over the building's proposed location behind the Joachimthal School on the Bundesallee. Finally, the 'Hauptstadt Berlin' competition in 1958 created the clear idea of a new cultural centre located on the edge of the Tiergarten, with a distinctive presence that could be combined with the old historic centre if the two parts of Berlin were re-united. In 1959 the Berlin Senate decided to move the Philharmonie site to the southern edge of the Tiergarten. Scharoun's concept of a 'musical centre' was not changed: all that was new was the opening up of the building and the arrangement of its elements. The first urban plan for the Tiergarten envisaged an elongated square, with the Matthaï Kirche at the top, buildings around the edges, and, as the asymmetrical conclusion of the square, the dynamic form of the Philharmonie with a small chamber music hall annexe.

The design of the Philharmonie was developed paradigmatically from inside out. Scharoun worked with the acoustic engineer Lothar Cremer to realize his idea of placing the podium in the centre of the concert hall. In the resulting asymmetrical space, only about ten per cent of the 2220 seats are positioned behind the orchestra: 600 seats are placed to the side, and terraced, in Scharoun's words, in the manner of a 'hillside vineyard'. The main seating is also raked in order to achieve the best possible acoustics. The result is an exemplary illustration of the idea of a community of listeners grouped around music. No concert-goer is more than 35 metres away from the podium.

The systematic opening up of the interior offers visitors a varied spatial experience – with stairs that cut through each other, a well-directed path of movement over various levels, and crystalline wall compartments. The foyers are related directly to the floor levels of the main hall. The main hall is also the major influence on the outer form of the Philharmonie. For many years, the exterior of the concert hall appeared unfinished and cold: lack of funds meant that the walls were concrete, painted ochre and white. Finally, in the 1980s, the building was clad in the way Scharoun had envisaged – with golden anodized aluminium panels that reflect the play of external light and the changing moods of the weather.

Competition model, Bundesallee site.

Design sketches.

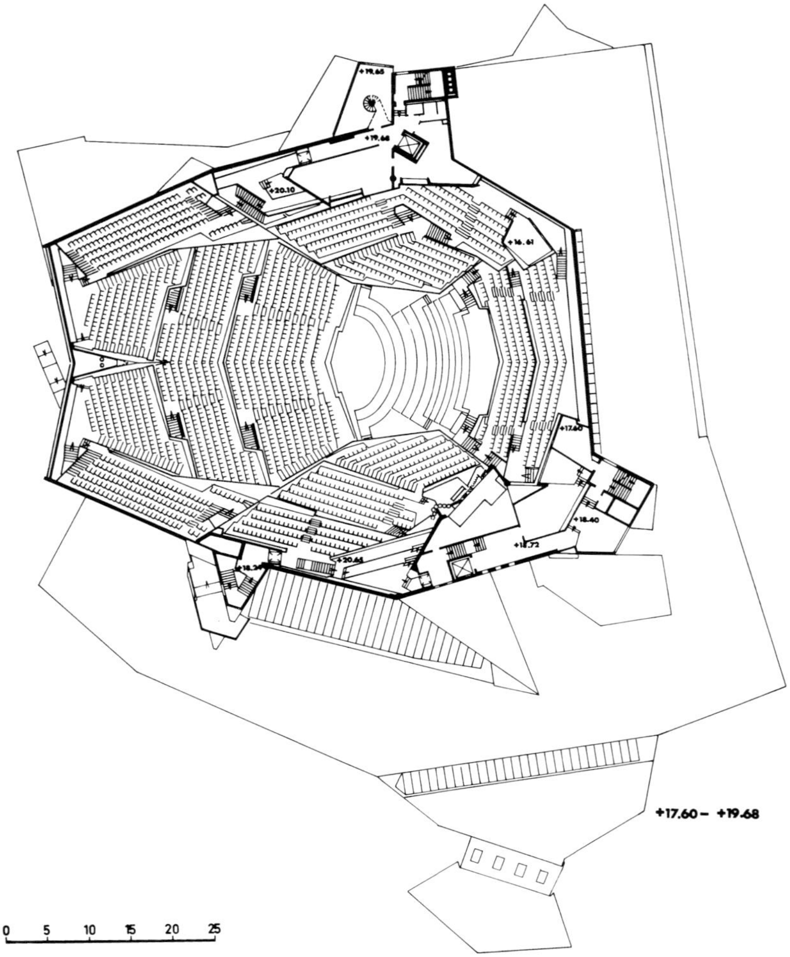

Plan and section of the concert hall.

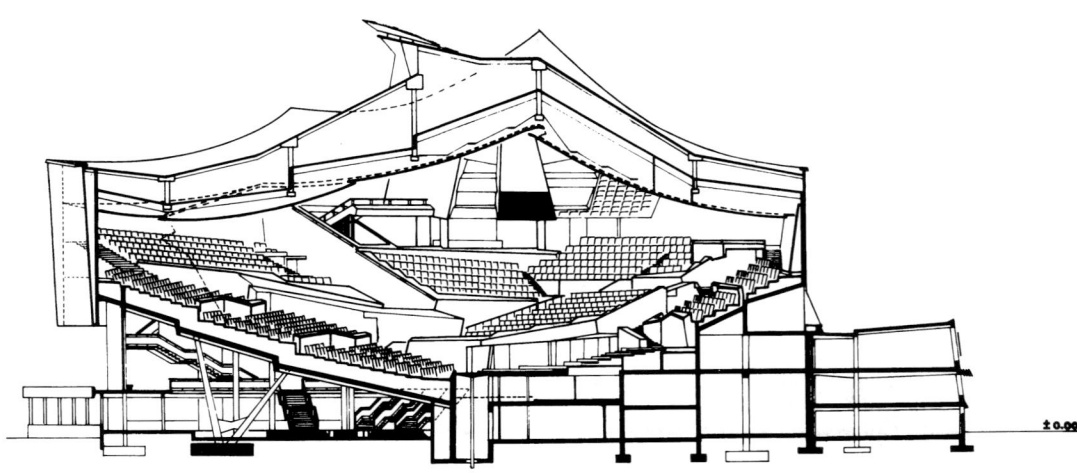

Model of the Philharmonie on the Matthäikirchplatz.

West elevation. Overleaf: concert hall of the Philharmonie.

1956–1962 The 'Geschwister Scholl' School, Lünen, Westphalia

With the girls' school in Lünen, Scharoun at last had the opportunity to apply the ideas on organic school building that he had developed in his 1952 design for an elementary school in Darmstadt.

The enclosed part of the school is set opposite the street and the Sacred Heart Church. It contains physics, biology and chemistry classrooms, accessible from a central, elongated hall. Opening towards the south are what Scharoun called 'classroom-homes'. The school is divided into lower, middle and upper sections following the Darmstadt model. In the south, the eight classrooms of the lower school are placed like a honeycomb around a circulation spine. The six middle classes are next to them and the four classrooms of the upper school are on the first floor across the hall. The circular playground is set by the side of the assembly hall. Further public areas are accessible from the semi-public spaces of the classroom gardens and the open-air teaching areas. Each 'classroom-home' consists of a classroom and common room, with an attached space for open-air lessons and a cloakroom. The size and orientation of the classrooms and open-air teaching areas are determined by the pupils' age and teaching requirements.

The arrangement and form of the rooms reflect Scharoun's attempt to create controllable areas which paralleled the development of the child while fostering growing independence. Individual and common areas interconnect and mingle, further encouraging pupils to identify with their school rooms and feel at home in them.

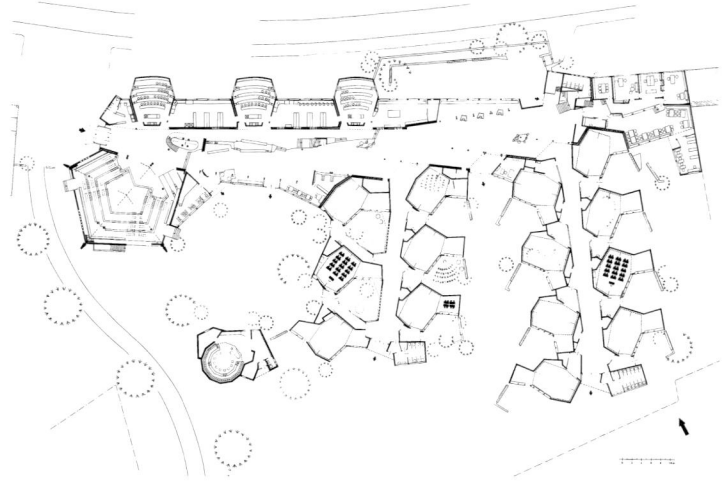

Ground-floor plan.

Right-hand page: bird's eye view from the southeast and view into the main hall.

129

1958 Hauptstadt Berlin
Competition entry, second prize, with Wils Ebert

The 'Hauptstadt Berlin' competition, launched on 30 March 1957 after many years of preparation, represented the last instance of CIAM's domination of the post-war debate in architecture. Otto Bartning held a key position on the competition committee, as he had in the Hansa district competition. He was joined by Werner Hebebrandt, Rudolf Hillebrecht and Hans Stephan. The jury included Alvar Aalto, Cornelis van Eesteren and Pierre Vago. Walter Gropius had declined to participate.

The most-discussed schemes – including the winner of the first prize – were striking applications of the principles of post-war CIAM urban planning to the city of Berlin. They were based on theories of the dispersed or fragmented city, and the idea of the ribbon city, in which the elements of the urban plan were ordered according to function. The centre of the city was rediscovered and consciously reformed as an identifiable space, in keeping with the theme of the 1951 CIAM Congress, the 'Heart of the City'.

Scharoun had already formulated precise planning principles for the central Berlin area in his 'collective plan' of 1946. Here he returned to the central idea of a 'city landscape' that would communicate a forceful image of the capital during the period of the cold war. The basically medieval structures of the city were to be combined with a modern traffic system in which various forms of movement were separated and horizontally layered to create the verdant, human-scaled city of tomorrow. Like others, Scharoun suggested that the government offices be moved to the Spreebogen, by the Reichstag. Urban axes were avoided, as they carried powerful associations with the recent past and with totalitarian regimes in general. This gave rise, amongst other things, to the asymmetrical form of the square in front of the Reichstag. The city's cultural facilities were 'anchors' which formed a 'spiritual band' forging links between the economic, political, residential and traffic areas in East and West. These facilities were not intended to be isolated on a central 'museum island', as they were in the Kulturforum on the Kemperplatz.

Scharoun expected the new identity of Berlin to evolve out of the opposition between the historical and the modern city, and this set his plan apart from the CIAM doctrine. His explanatory text states: 'The artistic task is new; artistic intuition will give this new undertaking

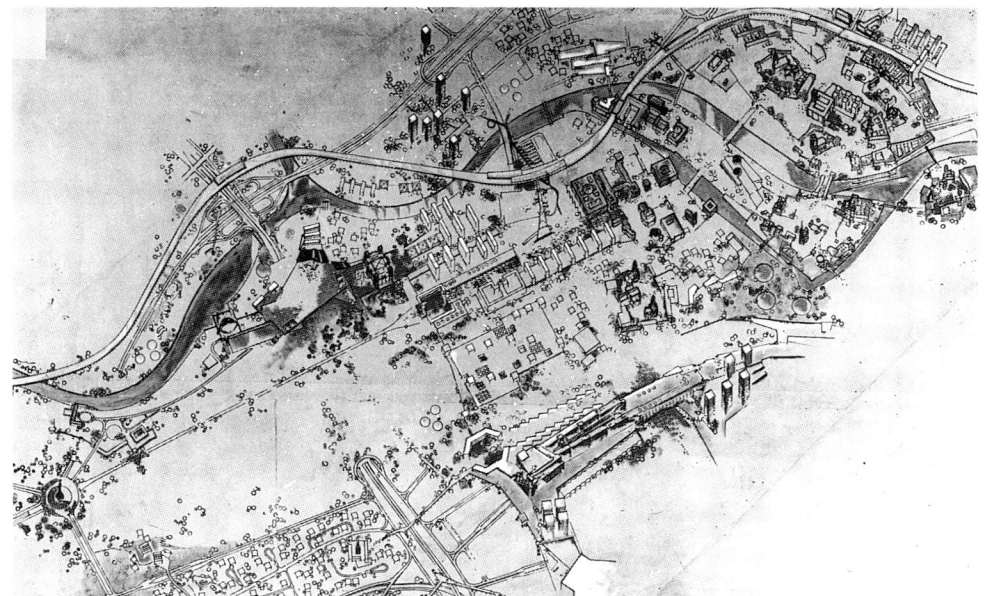

Competition entry, isometric representation.

the essential character and effect of the organic – without reference to style. This is in contrast to the structured methodology of place-making, which is bound up with the idea of the "State and Community of Berlin" and the traditional medieval core of Berlin. This brings into play the concept of "home", and requires a recognition of the existing landmarks in the city plan. The remains from the past set the tone here, for they bear witness to the roots from which the people and the city have come. This project therefore relates not only to the brief set by the City and the State of Berlin, but also to the fundamental psychological and spiritual "consolidation" that creates a sense of commonality – of belonging to a certain city.'

1960 Primary and Secondary School, Marl, Westphalia

In Marl, Scharoun had a further opportunity to express his thoughts on the organic school building. As in his earlier school in Lünen, the 'classroom-homes' are placed in a fan shape around a hall. In both the lower and middle schools, four classrooms are grouped in a single unit. Each classroom has an attached common room, lit from the side by a small atrium. The upper school (9th class) is placed in the centre of the complex and focused inwards towards the courtyards as an expression of inner concentration. At the centre of the recess hall is the assembly hall – a 'room in the middle' which is part of a sequence of terraced halls and courtyards, though it can be isolated if the need arises. The hall gives access to sports facilities, workshops, staffrooms, classrooms for natural/physical sciences and home economics, and the dining room. Here, too, Scharoun aimed to create a lively community: the school was an 'organically formed landscape', rather than an additive arrangement of buildings in an orthogonal grid.

Scharoun wrote: 'Marl takes up the ideas of Darmstadt, but in a form adapted to the specific natural and cultural circumstances. The classrooms and attendant hall are varied in a similar way [to the earlier project] ... The heart of the complex – this complex under one roof – is formed by the assembly place for the pupils, which serves not only as a recess hall but as a theatre, film or music room. This central room can be separated from the surrounding hall both spatially and acoustically – on a day-to-day basis, however, it remains tied to the complex as a whole so that all the children are aware of it and use it. It is not a closed-off "best room" but the focal point, indeed the soul of the whole place. This sense of unity is conveyed not only by the form of the roof but by the introduction of daylight into every part of the building. This includes the green spaces, both large and small, which punctuate the complex as a whole. The hall and the classrooms are connected in many ways to the external space. And despite the size of the complex as a whole, there is a clear attempt to achieve a rich variation of scale from the intimate to the ceremonial, always returning to the essence and scale of the child.'

Right-hand page: ground-floor plan.

Atrium.

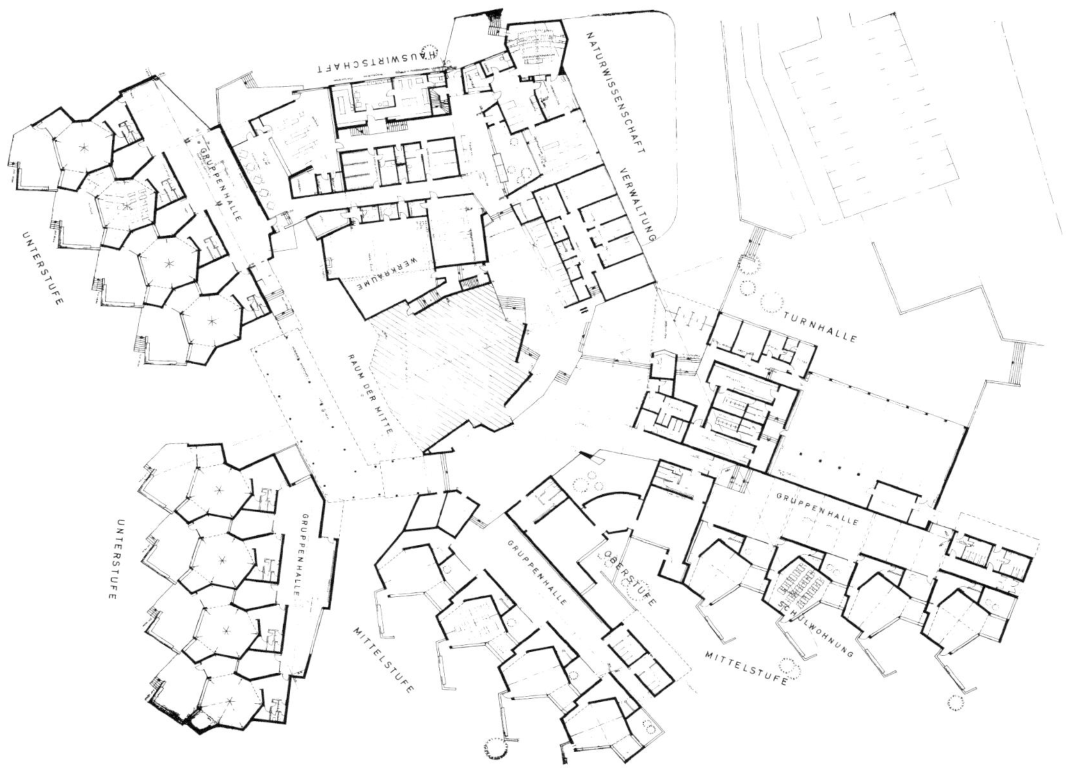
HAUSWIRTSCHAFT
NATURWISSENSCHAFT
VERWALTUNG
GRUPPENHALLE
UNTERSTUFE
WERKRÄUME
RAUM DER MITTE
TURNHALLE
GRUPPENHALLE
UNTERSTUFE
GRUPPENHALLE
GRUPPENHALLE
OBERSTUFE
SCHULWOHNUNG
MITTELSTUFE
MITTELSTUFE

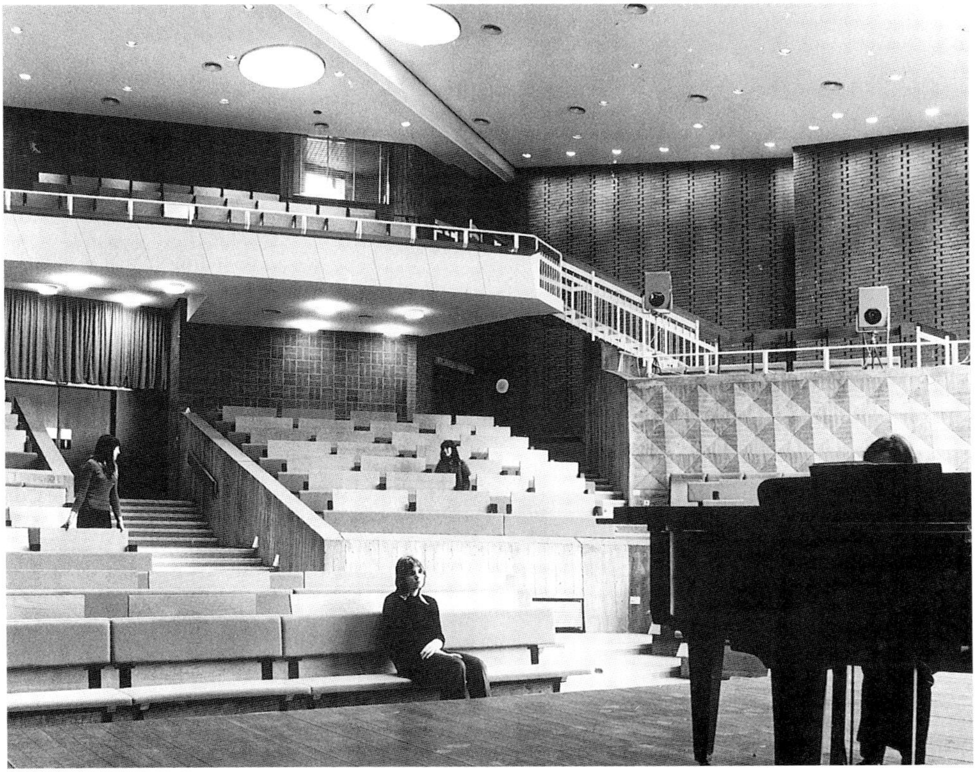

1961–1963 'Salute' high-rise, Stuttgart
With Wilhelm Frank

The design of the 'Salute' building in Stuttgart is similar in concept to the successful 'Romeo and Juliet' high-rises. It contains a total of 142 apartments. There are 15 different types, ranging from one room to six, from 42 square metres to 155, from one floor to two. All of the apartments are privately owned, but the broad variety of types ensures a broad social spectrum of occupants. The ground floor contains the caretaker's quarters and common facilities: a laundry room, storerooms, a crèche and a retail space. The lower part of the building has projecting balconies, but the upper part is stepped, and from the 17th floor large terraces are incorporated at various levels in the flat roof. The ground plan is divided into two sections either side of a line of circulation. This division achieves a relatively economical building form, while giving most apartments a dual aspect with a wide variety of views and little overlooking.

Typical floor plan (first floor). Right-hand page: 'Salute' high-rise.

1963/64 State Library for the Prussian Cultural Heritage Foundation, Berlin

Competition entry, first prize
In collaboration with Edgar Wisniewski, advised by Hermann Fehling
Landscape design: Hermann Mattern, Günther Nagel

The Library was built to provide a new home for the contents of the former Prussian State Library which had been dispersed during the war to Tübingen and Marburg. The design was the result of a limited competition amongst eleven architects: Scharoun (first prize), Gutbrod (second prize), Bornemann (commendation), Spengelin (commendation), Kramer/Seidel/Hausmann (special mention), Ruegenberg, Krahn, Seitz/Otto, Deilmann, Pfau and Ferdinand Kramer. The jury comprised P. Baumgarten, W. Düttmann, W. Hebebrand, B. Hermkes, R. Hillebrecht, H. Linde, C. Mertz, J. Rossig, K. Sage and H. Schwippert.

The Library was one of several buildings planned for the 'cultural band' of the Tiergarten. Its site was a cleared bomb site between Friedrich August Stüler's Matthäi Kirche, the already completed Philharmonie, and the Potsdamer Straße. Traffic planners proposed to run the Potsdamer Straße in front of the future State Library, to line up with the western approach to the Potsdamer Bridge. They also proposed to use the area to the rear of the State Library for an extension of the relief-road from the Tiergarten, effectively creating a 'western expressway'. The brief described this as a 'limited-access expressway, which will link the northern and southern areas of the city and connect with the other expressways and urban motorways.'

Scharoun proposed a grouping of individual buildings in the form of an 'urban landscape'. The longish mass of the State Library was to be shielded against the planned expressway in the west by the support spaces, store rooms and closed stacks. The reading rooms and other annexes were to step down towards the open ground of the Forum. The reading rooms pick up the cubic form of Mies's Nationalgalerie, while the terracing of the visitor's residence opposite responds to the form of the Forum. The plan also reiterates the idea of a defined square in front of the Matthäi Kirche – a 'piazza', in Scharoun's words – first formulated in the Philharmonie design.

In the interior, Scharoun created a quite unique spatial landscape that relates to the people who use the Library while meeting all functional requirements. Functional units, such as the various reading rooms, catalogue area and issue desk, are inserted into an organic continuous space, covered by a sun-screened ceiling which Scharoun called the 'skyscape'.

The technical complexity of the project led to difficulties on site, and in 1969 a second team was appointed to 'oversee the organization'. The construction process was largely the responsibility of Scharoun's long-time collaborator, Edgar Wisniewski. The building took 11 years to complete, and Scharoun did not live to see it open in December 1978. It cost a total of DM 23 million, and can house 2.8 million books.

The tragedy is that the State Library was planned to respond to an urban plan and traffic pattern that never materialized. Today, the expressway runs along the wrong side of the building, right next to the open areas of the Library. Perhaps the marking of the path of the multi-lane Neue Potsdamer Straße in the competition brief should have rung warning bells about the realities of the road-planners' schemes. The western expressway was planned to encourage a fast flow of traffic, unimpeded by intersections or bends. If, however, the road had been curved at this point, it could have joined up with the route of the old Potsdamer Straße – allowing the preservation of the old Potsdamer Bridge and, perhaps, the creation of a true forum for culture fronted by the Staatsgalerie. The reality is that the present road not only contains intersections and bends that slow down the motorist, but also destroys the character of the Forum and the urban landscape.

Sergius Ruegenberg was the only competition entrant to propose an alternative to the road scheme, placing the Neue Potsdamer Straße in an underground tunnel to create a square forum between the visitor's residence and the Library. His project was eliminated in the third round.

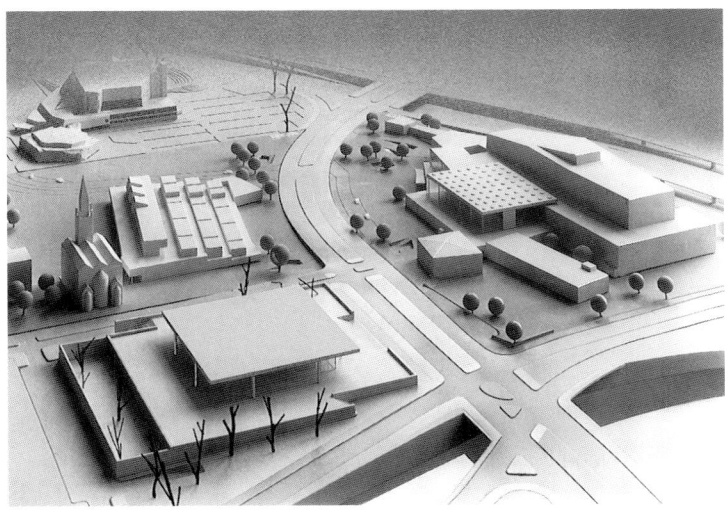

Competition model.

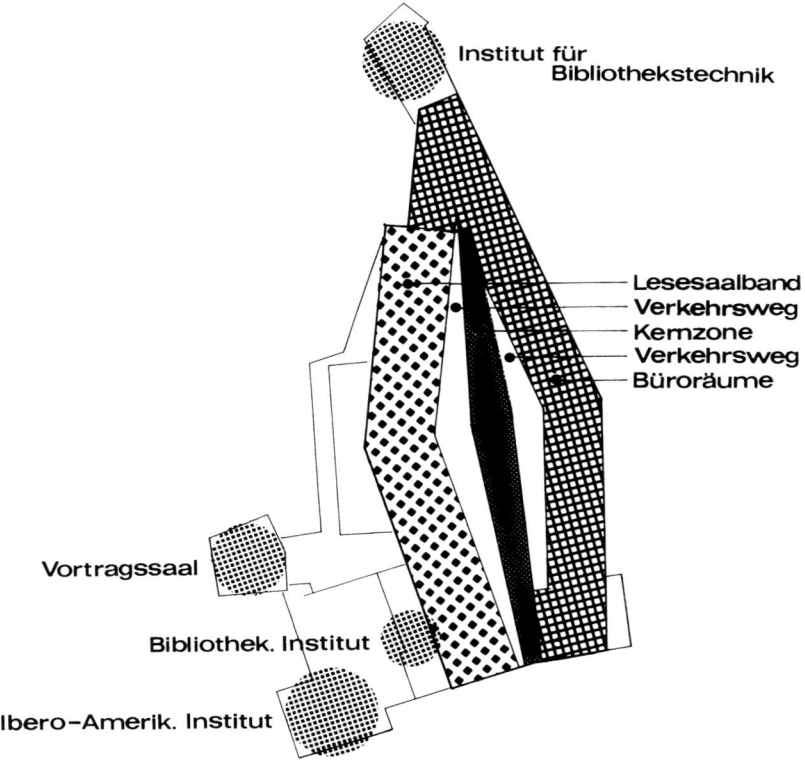

Diagram and plan of the ground-floor. Right-hand page: southwest elevation and view into the reading room.

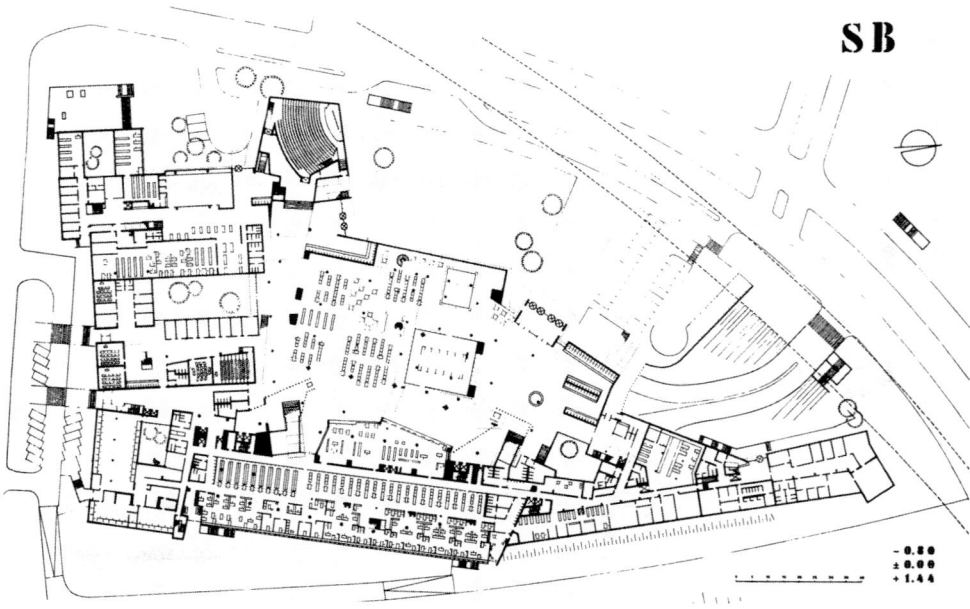

1964 German Embassy, Brasilia

In 1964 Scharoun was commissioned to design the embassy of the Federal Republic of Germany in Brasilia, the new capital of Brazil. Built between 1968 and 1971, this was his only work outside Germany.
The large complex contains the residence of the Ambassador, offices, public function rooms, accommodation for the Secretary and other personnel. In the southern portion of the lower floor are an exhibition space, a lecture hall, and the consulate. The north side contains the lower entrance to the public function rooms and the Ambassador's residence. The core of the complex is the four-storey chancellery. The entrance area connects first of all to the public function rooms and then to the small and large dining halls, forming a semicircle that matches the gentle slope of the site. The Ambassador's residence is placed in the northernmost part of the Embassy, behind the kitchen and service area.
In response to the equatorial climate, the outer form of the building incorporates wide roof overhangs, sun blinds and awnings. The red of the façades takes up the rust-red colour of the earth in the region. The Brazilian Roberto Burle Marx was responsible for the landscape design.

North elevation.

Overall view of Embassy.

Reception area with dining hall.

Plans of the first above-ground level of the Ambassador's Residence (left) and the staff area.

1965–1973   Municipal Theatre, Wolfsburg
Competition entry, first prize

Scharoun's success in the 1965 limited competition for the Wolfsburg Theatre was due in no small part to the composition of the jury, which included Werner Kallmorgen, Werner Düttmann and Rudolf Hillebrecht. The planning authorities at the time were also quite receptive to unconventional architecture, as the Alvar Aalto buildings in the city make clear. Indeed, Aalto won the second prize in the competition: two joint third prizes were awarded to Spengelin and Taescher/Gerdes; three joint fourths to Utzon, Bornemann and Schramm/Pempelfort. The building, inaugurated in 1973, was Scharoun's only executed theatre design.

The theatre stands on the northern slope of the Klieverberg not far from the southern end of the Porschestraße. The primary elevation – as designated by Scharoun – extends from the foyer in the southeast to the administrative area in the northwest, placing the theatre in full view of the city. Viewed from the east, the theatre aligns itself with the hill which rises away from the city hall. From the south it consists of a loose sequence of buildings distributed around the slope of the hill, forming a focal point for the inner city – a city 'crown'. The theatre is framed against the backdrop of a wooded hilltop; in the foreground lies a gentle green slope.

The northeast façade is determined by two ordering schemes which divide the theatre horizontally into two levels. The lower level covers a third of the total height and contains the administrative area and foyer. It forms a visually continuous band clad with light travertine, terminating in an aluminium string course. The second level covers the upper two-thirds of the building. It contains the stage and auditorium area, and is clad in grey granite.

Vertically, the building is divided into three parts: the foyer; the stage and auditorium; the administrative and cloakroom area. To the left is the freely formed mass of the foyer. The interior of the foyer is an elongated space consisting of sharp angles, roofs and projections which appear random, but in fact follow distinct ordering systems, creating a lively spatial experience.

Rising next to this is the crystalline, grey mass of the fly-tower and auditorium. The outer angular form of the building mass expresses the division between stage and auditorium. The sides contain alternating obtuse and acute angles, which clearly express the internal volume – an effect reinforced by the play of light and shade across the façade.

Approaching the auditorium, the visitor comes first of all to an intermediate level, with access left and right to the stalls and circle. A central opening leads to the rear boxes – reflecting the original intention of dividing the stalls into two. From the circle to the stage, the auditorium has a clear symmetrical arrangement. Only the asymmetrical division of the circle hints at the arrangement of the seating in the competition entry. The moveable proscenium is drawn forward to meet the stalls and comes to an obtuse angle in the middle. The seating reflects this angle in its symmetrical arrangement about a central axis. The ceiling rises steeply from the stage up to the first row of the circle and then drops gradually towards the external glazed area to the rear. Near the stage, the ceiling contains deeply recessed acoustic reflectors, which also support the stage lighting, giving an extended reflective void. Combined with the remaining lamps, which are simply inset into the ceiling, this creates an animated 'starry sky'.

Competition entry, ground plan.

Design sketch of foyer.

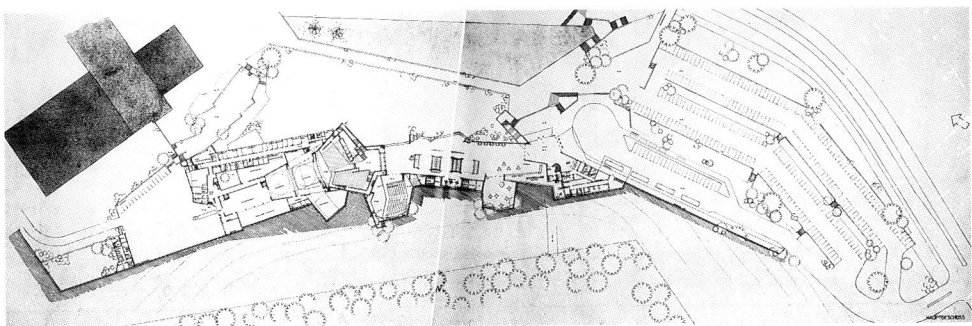

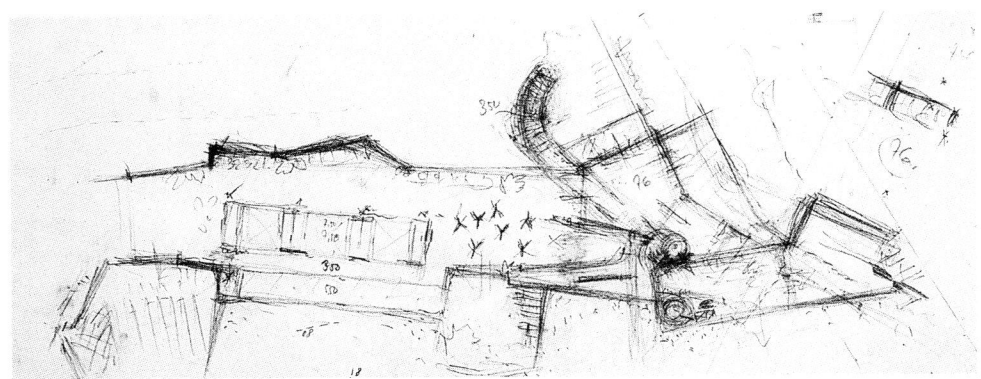

Northeast elevation.

Plan of administrative area, stage and auditorium.

Lobby with view into the auditorium and stairs to circle.

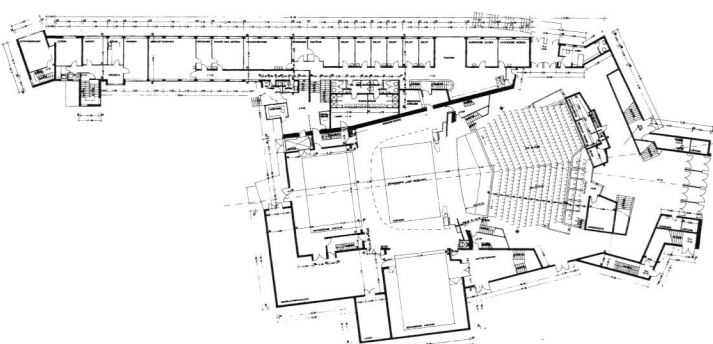

1965/66 Chapel of St. John for the Community of Christ in Glockengarten, Bochum

With Gundolf Bockemühl

The commission to design the Chapel of the Community of Christ in Bochum – Scharoun's only built ecclesiastical work – stemmed from the daughter of one of his early clients, Fritz Schminke. The Anthroposophical church was consecrated on 10 December 1966.
The small building sits next to a neo-classical manor house, which today serves as the rectory. The seating is arranged symmetrically about a long axis, but the symmetry is disturbed by the flanking walls which are set at obtuse angles to each other. The sacristy in the southeast corner is balanced by a music room in the northwest corner. The inward-leaning south wall is pierced by an elongated triangular window with diamond-shaped glazing. Further small, triangular windows are placed at the oblique angles of the walls, bringing diaphanous light into a rather dark space. Elements of the ceiling, which is simply clad in wood, converge in front of the altar space at a point corresponding to the crossing. The higher ceiling over the altar allows for the effective use of top light. The west wall of the ante-room, next to the entrance, supports a low bell tower. Scharoun drew several variants of the bell tower, showing a higher free-standing form, with an oblique end wall, supporting both free-hanging bells and large free-standing acoustic devices. The calm, almost sombre tones of the interior are continued on the exterior, with the grey slate, the dark clinker brick, the wood and the continuous coping band, which Scharoun intended to be of copper.
Scharoun designed a building in keeping with the formal vocabulary of Anthroposophical architecture, with deep overhangs and a broad ledge tied directly to the roof. However the chapel also bears his own distinctive signature, relating in a formal sense not only to contemporary work but also, with its sheltering, folded roofscape, quite directly to early Expressionist-crystalline designs.

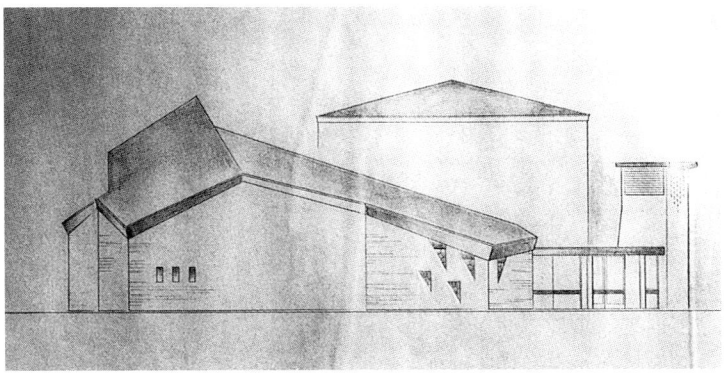

Elevation.

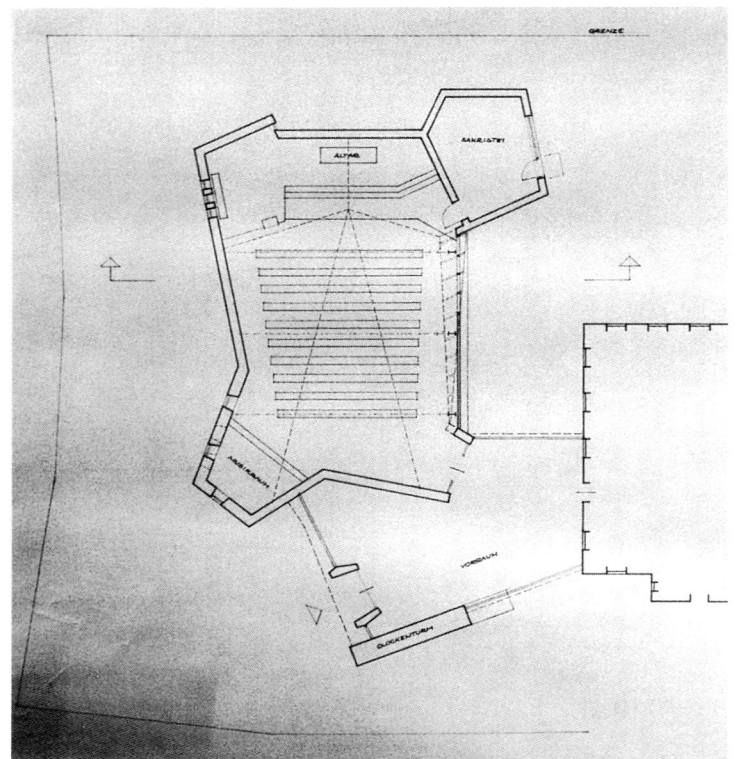

Ground plan.

North elevation.

Right-hand page: view of the altar.

View from the altar.

1966 Church of the Transfiguration of Christ, Berlin-Schöneberg
Project

The proposed site for the Church of the Transfiguration of Christ was the edge of the Viktoria-Luise-Platz in Berlin-Schöneberg, at the point where the Motzstraße and the Winterfeldstraße joined the plaza. Scharoun designed a small wedge-shaped building, which related to the corner site and the asymmetrical form of the five-cornered plaza as a whole. The plan also recalls the Wolfsburg Theatre designed a short time earlier. The bell tower is placed in the centre of the square, separate from the church, so that it can be seen, and heard, from all the streets leading into the square. The tower also marks the entrance to the subway.
The lower floor contains the crypt, a large parish room and the supply rooms. The main floor is connected to the square by a bridge. On entering the church, the visitor's attention is focused beyond the seating – which is divided in two about a slightly curving axis – towards the altar. From the entrance area, a spiral stair to the left leads up to the gallery, while a passage to the right goes to a baptismal apse and an enclosed crèche. The space is defined by the visible concrete support structure, which carries the stepped ceiling elements on its cantilevered arms. The structure is meant to symbolize the 'tree of life'. Such overt symbols, otherwise rare in Scharoun's work, are freely used in his ecclesiastical projects. The interior also contains the same triangular, for the most part right-angled windows that are found in the Chapel of St. John of the Community of Christ in Bochum, designed two months earlier. The motif of the triangle is repeated in the roof segments, the structure and the walls, forming an architectural and a symbolic unity. The glazing and the small high windows set in the compartmentalized roof give the interior an unusual diaphanous lighting reminiscent of Gothic churches.
This project shows the contribution Scharoun would have been able to make to the genre – if he had ever had the opportunity to build a large church.

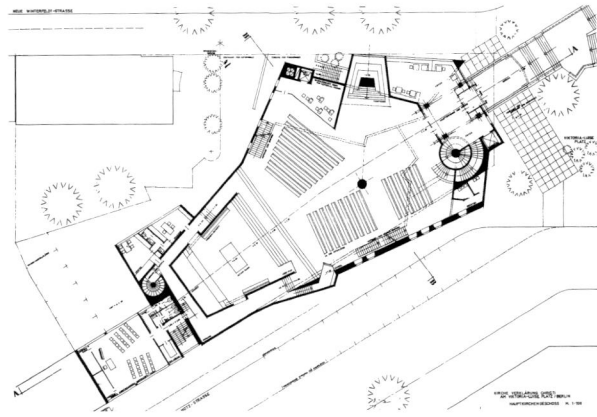

Plan of main floor.

Model of the church with Viktoria-Luise Platz.

Load-bearing structure of the 'tree of life'.

1969 Protestant church and community centre, Wolfsburg-Rabenberg
'Haus der offenen Tür' (Open house) design

Scharoun's projects in Wolfsburg included not only the Municipal Theatre but also unbuilt designs for a community centre and kindergarten.
The community centre and church form an enclosed area, arranged like a medieval castle around an inner courtyard and garden. In the centre is the spatial focus of the design – a cylindrical, top-lit baptistry which opens onto the church on one side, and the garden on the other. The baptistry leads north to the church, via a gallery and an extendable hall that can be linked with the club room. In the east is the chancellery with a hexagonal lantern which brings in top light and marks the position of the altar. Also to the east is the home of the parish priest. Many of the spaces, including the church itself, open on to the large courtyard garden to the south. The southern edge of the complex is marked by the triangular bell tower, which contains the entrance to the enclosure. As visitors pass through this modern interpretation of the old gatehouse, they are made thoroughly aware of the process of 'entering'. They are led through the courtyard, from where they have a view of the whole complex, then into the western cloakroom and foyer area, approaching only slowly the inner area of the church and baptistry. This project represents a throughly individual, innovative approach to community centre design. The spatial relations are formally differentiated, as required by the brief, but none the less ordered in a functional manner. The roofs are mainly of a shallow monopitch and are divided into single segments, creating a crystalline volume that symbolizes both shelter and divine exaltation.

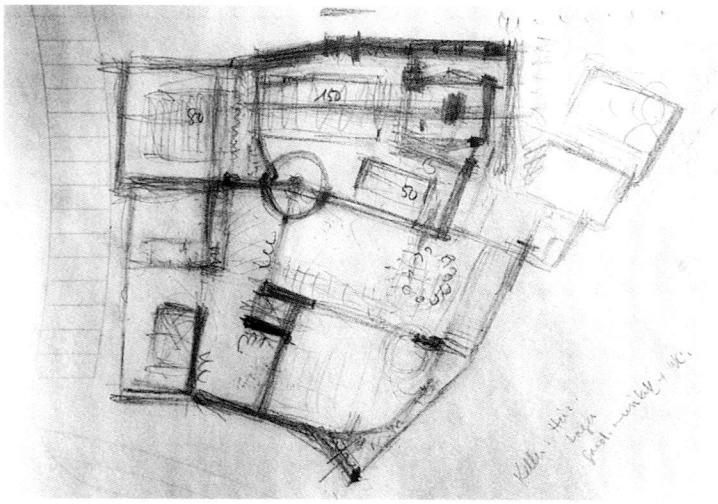

Design sketch.
Right-hand page:
ground-floor plan and
model.

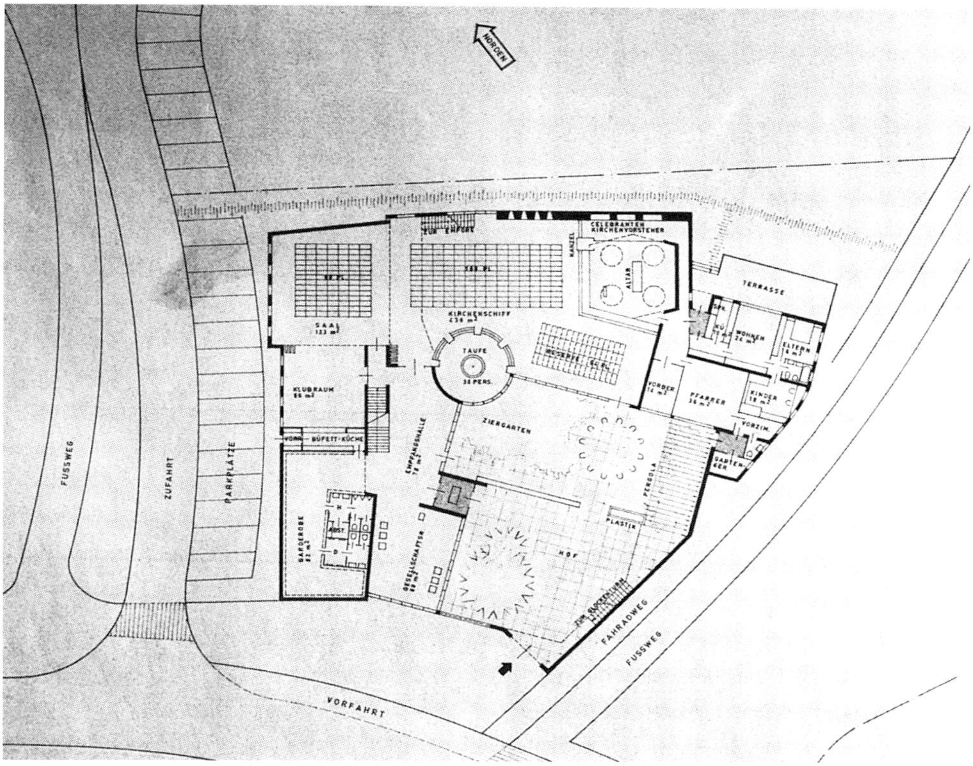
NORDEN
ZUR EMPORE
CELEBRANTEN
KIRCHENVORSTEHER
KANZEL
ALTAR
TERRASSE
SAAL
KIRCHENSCHIFF
TAUFE
WOHNEN
ELTERN
KLUBRAUM
VORBER
PFARRER
KINDER
VORZIM.
VORR.
BÜFETT-KÜCHE
ZIERGARTEN
EMPFANGSHALLE
GARTEN-
GER.
PERGOLA
PLASTIK
GARDEROBE
GESELLSCHAFTSR.
HOF
ZUM GLOCKENTURM
FAHRADWEG
FUSSWEG
ZUFAHRT
PARKPLÄTZE
VORFAHRT

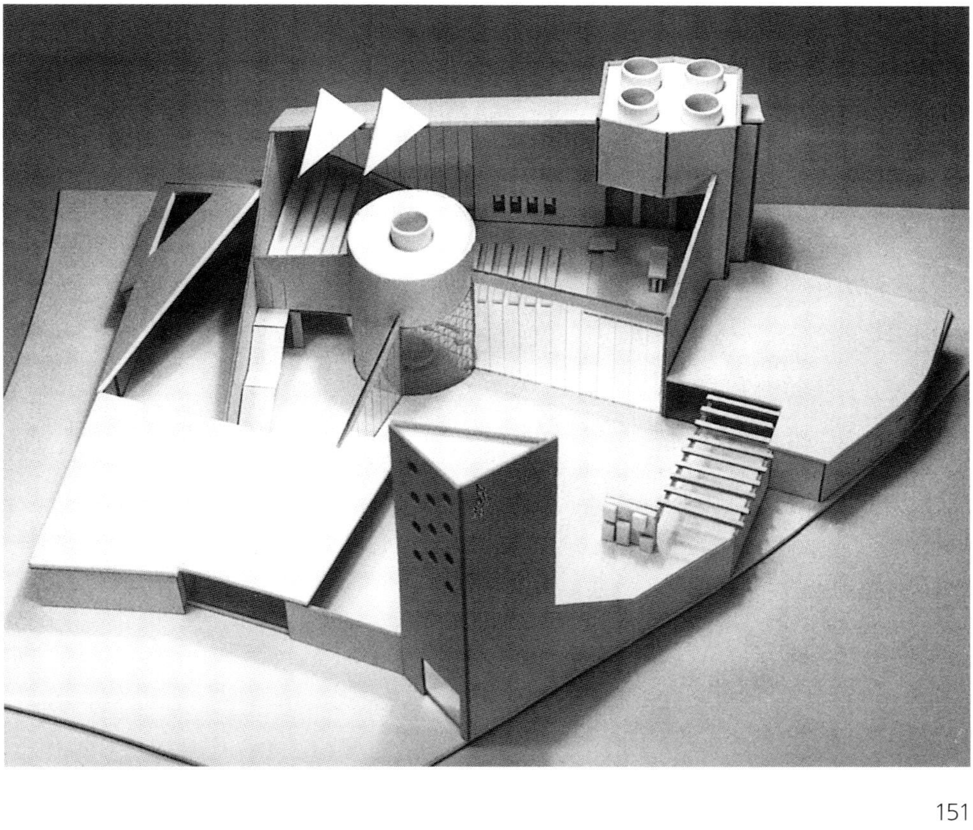

1970 German Maritime Museum, Bremerhaven
With Helmut Bohnsack

Towards the end of his life, Scharoun received a commission to build a maritime museum in the city in which he had spent his childhood. The new building was to house a spectacular archaeological find – a Hanseatic cog sailboat discovered in 1962, but ready for display only after a 20-year process of conservation.

The Museum lies between the Weser river and the old harbour, and steps down parallel to the Weser dyke. In keeping with Scharoun's principles of design, the individual functional areas are clearly marked by the changes of level, but at the same time are brought together in a meaningful composition. The linking middle area houses the navigation exhibition. It leads on one side to the southern part of the complex, and on the other to the room set aside for the display of the Hanseatic cog.

The architect's explanatory text states: 'The variety inherent in the design, which is expressed in the structure and form of the building, also mirrors the essential character of its natural and cultural environment. It reflects the harbour city and the people who work in it – the special activities that are repeatedly demanded of people for the purpose of achieving and securing constantly changing goals . . .

'The power of intuition has accompanied my design work since my early youth. Thus it is a special pleasure to be allowed to plan the German Maritime Museum in Bremerhaven – where I first discovered the interest in form that has motivated me all my life. In the Maritime Museum, I have responded to the many practical problems of construction with a similarly complex functional ordering that comprises not only the building itself but also the arrangement of the objects in the open-air museum in the park and Old Harbour. Intimacy alternates with vistas, with views in and out. The multimedia approach to the research and display of the collection will brings to life an important part of the history of the ship and its world . . .

'The division of tasks and the creation of focal points will act to order the whole building and its environment – which formerly marked the border between East and West – and communicate to the viewer a formal enclosure precisely enveloping the content of the building.'

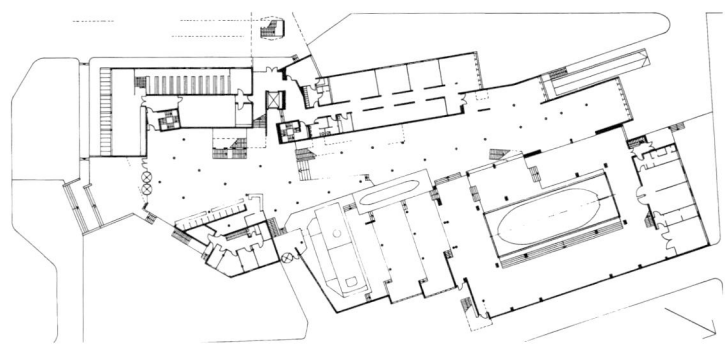

Ground-floor plan.

Model from east.

West elevation.

Southeast elevation.

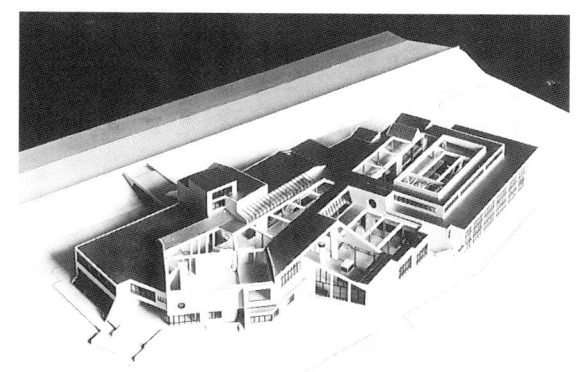

1969–1971 State Institute for Musical Research and Museum of Instruments, Berlin-Tiergarten

Work-cooperative with Edgar Wisniewski

The construction and interior design of the Institute for Musical Research and Museum of Instruments was undertaken by Scharoun's office after his death. The commission for the new building came in 1969, and Scharoun prepared the design himself. But the construction phase began only in 1978, some six years after his death.
The building is divided functionally into two. The square mass of the Institute for Musical Studies sits parallel to the Philharmonie, whilst the elongated Museum of Instruments extends to the corner of the Tiergartenstraße and Potsdamer Straße. As in the museum at Bremerhaven, the heart of the building consists of a meeting space, surrounded by two levels of exhibition space divided into small, thematically arranged rooms all open along one side. Visitors standing on the galleries are also able to enjoy the musical performances in the central space. The interiors of the Museum, however, are at times displeasingly overdone, counteracting the delicacy of the musical instruments on display. The scheme remains faithful on the surface to the details of Scharoun's formal vocabulary, but manages to quote it into sterility.
The building was opened in December 1984.

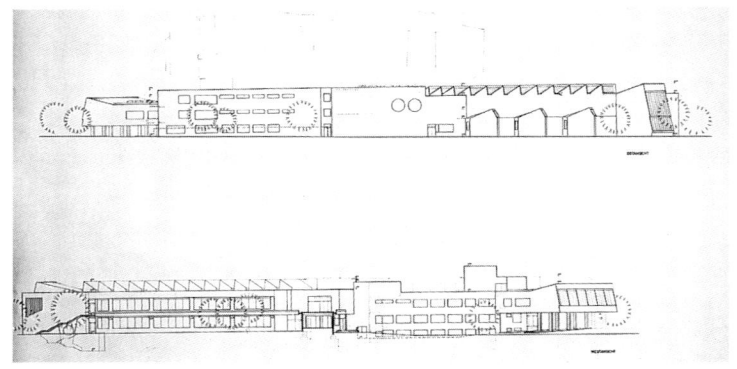

Elevations.

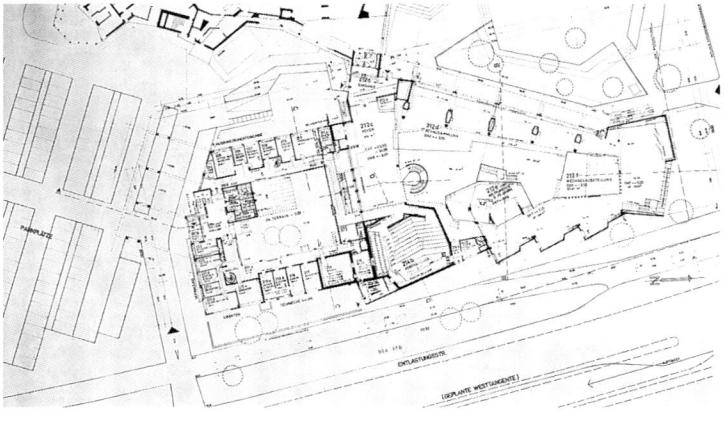

Ground-floor plan.

1968–1971 Chamber Music Hall for the Philharmonie, Berlin-Tiergarten
Design sketch: Hans Scharoun
Design and execution: Edgar Wisniewski

The Chamber Music Hall for the Philharmonic Orchestra provoked a debate about the authenticity of Scharoun's posthumously built works. The building was inaugurated in the summer of 1988, some 20 years after the initial planning. The passage of time alone gave rise to many changes: for once, the 'evolution of the built form in space and time' turned against Scharoun, becoming merely a laconic justification for a formalistic approach to the design process. Scharoun provided only a design sketch showing the spatial concept – a reapplication of the Philharmonie's principle of 'music in the centre' to a smaller, more intimate space. The sketch shows an axially symmetrical central space, with a hexagonal podium for the musicians and curving stepped segments for the auditorium. The idea of 'music in the centre' is interpreted literally: the audience is arranged evenly in a circle and not distributed in various ways around the podium, as in the Philharmonie.

Scharoun's 1959 design for the Berlin Philharmonie showed the chamber-music annexe to the south of the main building. The intention was to terminate visually the projecting line of

Design sketch. Overleaf: Kulturforum, from left to right: Chamber Music Hall, Philharmonie, and the State Institute for Musical Research with the Museum of Instruments.

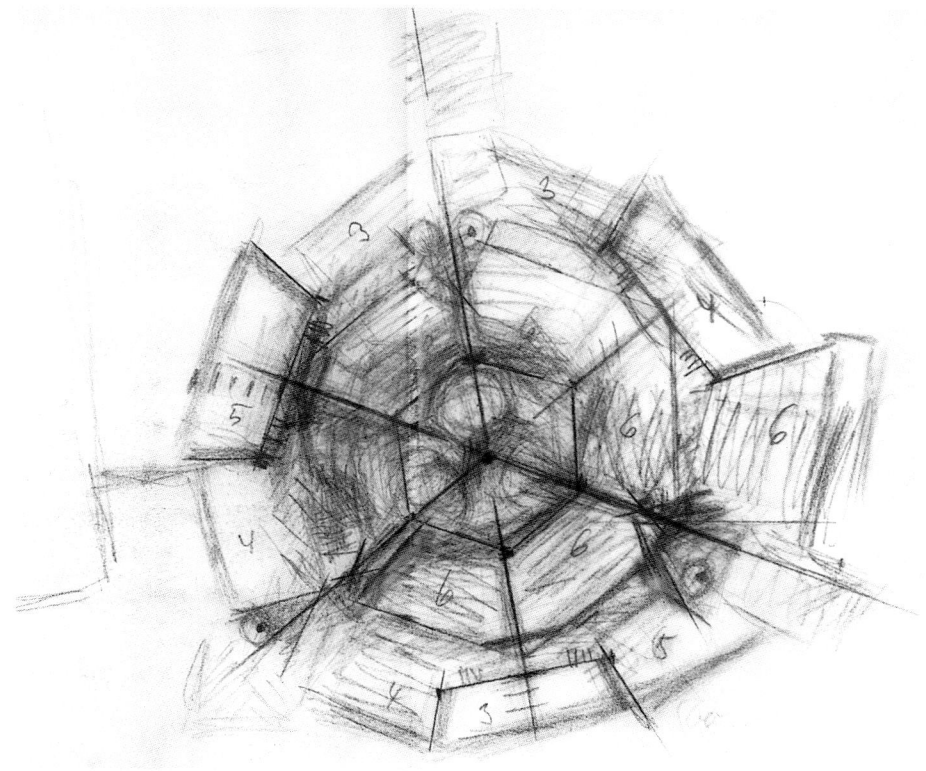

the Philharmonie and at the same time to establish a connection with the surrounding buildings on the piazza between the Matthäi Kirche and the Philharmonie. In the course of planning, however, the volume of the Chamber Music Hall swelled many times over, partly because of the client's requirements, partly because of the musicians' increased need for space, and partly because of the architect's ambition. The building also grew unfortunately tall in relation to its overall size. The lower level contains the foyers (like the Philharmonie, only bigger) and the mechanical and support spaces (unlike the Philharmonie, where they are housed in separate annexes).

The Chamber Music Hall turned out to be almost as big as the Philharmonie, with seating for 1189 'only'. Although it functions well, it cannot be seen as an annexe to or spatial complement of the Philharmonie. The two buildings appear equal, with the Chamber Music Hall repeating by rote the language of Scharoun. Here, we see one more permanent change to Scharoun's original plan for the Kulturforum – and a clear illustration why further experiments of this nature should be avoided once and for all.

Elevation.

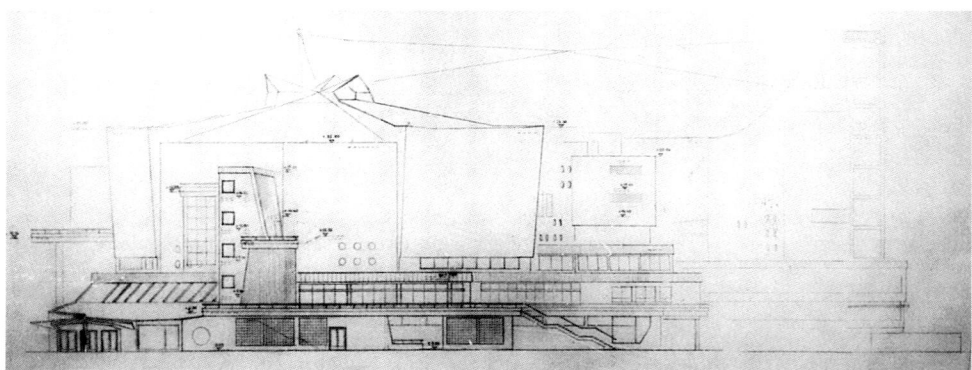

Appendix

Biography

1893
Bernhard Hans Henry Scharoun was born on 20 September 1893 in Bremen. His family surname had been changed from the Bohemian 'Saraun' by his great-grandfather, Vaclav Saraun, when he became a citizen of Bremen in 1816. Vaclav Saraun was born in 1788 in Solnice, Bohemia, and was a shoemaker by trade. Scharoun's grandfather, Bernhard, was a regional postmaster in Bremerhaven and the father of nine children.
Scharoun's father, Bernhard Emil, was born in Bremen in 1861 and was first a merchant and then the director of a brewery in Bremerhaven. He married in 1889: Scharoun's mother came from Lüneburg, from an old family of craftsmen. Scharoun spent his childhood in Bremerhaven: he had two brothers, one older, one younger, who both died in the First World War. His father died in 1911, his mother in 1943.
Contemporary documents point to an orderly, solid middle-class family life. But there were certain tensions between Scharoun and his father, who tried to stifle his interests in drawing and building. The young Scharoun had to turn for support to some liberal neighbours: the family of an architect and builder called Hoffmeyer, who made an effort to link the boy's ideas with the realities of the profession.
While still at school, Scharoun entered his first architectural competition, presenting a design for a church in Bremerhaven which attempted to establish fundamental links between 'land and sea'.

1912
Finished school in Bremerhaven.

1912–1914
Studied in the Faculty of Architecture at the Technische Hochschule of Berlin-Charlottenburg.

1915–1918
Scharoun volunteered for the army in 1914 and joined the artillery after Crossen an der Oder. From 1915 to 1918 he was assigned to a military construction command within East Prussia itself. He was second-in-command: the captain was his friend and mentor Paul Kruchen, who had tutored at the Technische Hochschule in Berlin. Scharoun drew up watchtowers and fortifications for prisoner-of-war camps. With the help of Scharoun's decorative drawings Kruchen was able to gain rapid authorization for his plans. After an initial period in Gumbinnen, Scharoun went with Kruchen to Insterburg. At the end of the war Scharoun returned to Berlin to resume his studies at the Technische Hochschule. He hoped that his proven experience and achievements would enable him to move directly into the upper

school. Instead, he was asked to take the preliminary examination – so he went right back to East Prussia and took up Kruchen's former government post as an independent architect.

1919–1925
Private practice in Insterburg, East Prussia. Member of the 'Crystal Chain' group around Bruno Taut, producing numerous Expressionist drawings and watercolours, primarily for social and cultural buildings.

1920
Married Anna Marie Hoffmeyer.

1925–1932
Professor at the State Academy for Arts and Crafts, Breslau.
The Academy was created in 1911 out of the Breslau School of Art. Its first Director was Hans Poelzig. He was followed by August Endell and then Oskar Moll, who invited Scharoun to Breslau. Scharoun's best-known work during this period is his housing for the Werkbund Exhibition, 'Wohnung und Werkraum' (Wuwa), in Breslau in 1929; other notable works were the house in the Weissenhofsiedlung, Stuttgart, and the Siemensstadt *Siedlung* in Berlin.

1926
Architectural practice with Paul Kruchen and Adolf Rading in Berlin.
Founder-member of the 'Ring', which initially comprised: Bartning, Behrens, Häring, Mendelsohn, Mies van der Rohe, Poelzig, Schilbach, B. Taut and M. Taut. One of the Ring's main aims was to combat the conservative policies of the City's Director of Building, Ludwig Hoffmann. On 29 May 1926 the loose association became an official architectural group, with Hugo Häring as Secretary and 28 members – all of them, including Scharoun, representatives of the New Architecture. The Ring Group was banned in 1933.
Martin Wagner appointment as Berlin's Director of Building in 1926 opened up opportunities for Scharoun – in the form of competitions, commissions for planning reports, and, in 1930, work on the Siemensstadt *Siedlung*.

1932–1945
Private practice in Berlin.
In 1932 the Breslau Academy was closed as part of an austerity package formulated by Chancellor Brüning, and in 1933 Scharoun found that he was denied government work. Unlike others, he did not emigrate, but turned instead to private clients, building around 20 single-family homes in the years up to 1942.
During the war Scharoun worked on a research project on laundry facilities and on clearing the damage caused by aerial bombardment. He also produced countless watercolours which depicted his vision of a future architecture: 'Each day, from the outbreak of the war until the final surrender, he made drawings, watercolours, designs, partly out of a need to keep himself occupied, partly out of a need to address the issue of future form.'

1945/46
Director of Building and Housing for the Municipal Authority of Greater Berlin. The exhibition 'Berlin plans' (22 August 1946) introduced the principles of an 'urban landscape' that was to form the basis of his later urban plans.

1946–1958
Taught in the Faculty of Architecture at the Technische Universität of Berlin.

1947–1950
Head of the Institute of Building Science at the German Academy of Sciences in Berlin. Scharoun continued to develop his plans for Berlin, seeing the reconstruction of the Friedrichshain quarter as an ideal opportunity to realize a prototypical urban 'neighbourhood'. This never happened: his ideas were made unworkable by the planning of the Stalinallee and his employment at the Institute of Building Science came to an end.
During this time Scharoun attempted to regroup the architects who had been involved in the New Architecture before the war. A German CIAM Group was planned and the 'Ring' Group refounded.

1951–1956
In 1951 Scharoun produced a design for an elementary school in Darmstadt which was presented at a colloquium on 'People and Space'. This project, together with others in the 1950s – the Kassel Theatre project (1952), 'Romeo and Juliet' high-rises (1954) and Philharmonie (1956) – represented the fundamental stages in Scharoun's development of an organic architecture, the 'spiritual basis of building, the structure in space and time'.

1954
Fritz Schumacher Prize from the Freiherr vom Stein Foundation in Hamburg.
Honorary doctorate from the Technische Hochschule, Stuttgart.
Berlin Prize for Art.

1955
Member of the Academy of Arts, Berlin.

1955–1968
President of the Academy of Arts, Berlin.

1956
Member of the advisory council on planning to the Senator for Building and Housing, Berlin.

1959
Awarded Order of the Federal Republic of Germany.
Honoured by the Free Academy of Arts, Hamburg.

1960
Married the journalist Margit von Plato.

1962
Honorary Senator of the Technische Universität, Berlin.

1964
Gold Medal from the German Institute of Architects.

1965
Auguste Perret Prize from the UIA.
Honorary doctorate from the University of Rome.

1968
Became Honorary President of the Academy of Arts, Berlin.
Gold Medal for Architecture from the State of North Rhine-Westphalia.

1969
Made Honorary Citizen of Berlin.

1970
Praemium Erasmianum.

1971
Fellow of the Académie d'Architecture, Paris.
Honorary member of the Colegio de Arquitectos de Peru.

1972
Died on 25 November in Berlin.

Notes

1 Wolfgang Pehnt, Expressionist Architecture, London 1973, p. 102.
2 Cf. Franco Borsi, Giovanni Klaus König, Architettura dell'espressionismo, Genoa 1967.
3 Peter Blundell Jones, Hans Scharoun: A Monograph, London/Bedford 1979.
4 Carl Claussen, 'Insterburger Nachrichten', 14 November 1925, in Peter Pfankuch (ed.), Hans Scharoun, Bauten, Entwürfe, Texte, Akademie der Künste, Berlin 1974.
5 Ibid.
6 Max Berg, 'Der Berliner Hochhauswettbewerb', in Bauwelt, no. 8, 1922, p. 125f.
7 Adolf Behne to Scharoun, 8 June 1923, quoted in Pfankuch, op. cit., p. 38.
8 Adolf Behne, Der moderne Zweckbau, Munich 1926, p. 48.
9 G. A. Platz, Die Baukunst der neuesten Zeit, Berlin 1927, p. 136.
10 Scharoun, 14 January 1968, in Pfankuch, op. cit., p. 144: 'We need many outside influences and help if we are to fulfil our ideas and creations in this world—as I came fully to realize through my meetings with Erich Mendelsohn.'
11 Scharoun, 1948, 'Die T.U.', No. 2/3, 1949, in Pfankuch, op. cit., p. 177.
12 One example was a talk on the 'Crystal Chain' on Free Berlin Radio on 14 March 1964: see Pfankuch, op. cit., p. 15: 'This was the beginning of "organic building", which was based on the thinking of Hugo Häring. In place of "form-setting", there was "form-finding". In place of the premise of architectonic elements, there was structural order—the essential representation of an "event" in the functional and spiritual sense.'
13 Hugo Häring, 'strukturprobleme des bauens', manuscript of a lecture, 1946, in Heinrich Lauterbach, Jürgen Joedicke, Hugo Häring, Schriften, Entwürfe, Bauten, Stuttgart 1965, p. 50.
14 Hugo Häring, 'wege zur form', Die Form, issue 1, October 1925.
15 Ibid.
16 Cf. Pehnt, op. cit., p. 200.
17 Hugo Häring, 'wege zur form', op. cit.
18 Hugo Häring, 'proportionen', Deutsche Bauzeitung, no. 29, 18 July 1934, quoted in Lauterbach, Joedicke, op. cit., p. 35.
19 Hugo Häring, 'probleme der stilbildung', Deutsche Bauzeitung, no. 43, 24 October 1934, quoted in Lauterbach, Joedicke, op. cit., p. 36.
20 Ibid. p. 37.
21 Ibid. p. 39.
22 Hans Bernhard Reichow, Organische Stadtbaukunst, Braunschweig 1948.
23 Hugo Häring, 'betrachtungen über den zweifelhaften wert des gesunden menschenverstandes', manuscript 1947, in Lauterbach, Joedicke, op. cit., p. 64.
24 Cf. Hans Scharoun, in a manuscript quoted in Peter Pfankuch (ed.), Hans Scharoun, Berlin 1974, p. 151.
25 Letter from W. Gropius to H. Scharoun, 12 July 1946, Gropius Papers, Houghton Library, Harvard.
26 P. Pfankuch, op. cit.
27 The group comprised, in addition to Scharoun: Karl Böttcher, Wils Ebert, Peter Friedrich, Ludmilla Herzenstein, Reinhold Lingner, Luise Seitz and Herbert Weinberger. Ebert had represented Gropius at the CIAM Congress in Athens, where he had presented a project on Berlin. Selmanagic joined Gropius's practice in 1932 and was involved with the planning of the 1933 CIAM Congress. See: Johann Friedrich Geist, Klaus Kürvers, Das Berliner Mietshaus, 1945–1989, Munich 1989.
28 H. Scharoun, 'Vom Wesen der Stadt', in Der Tagesspiegel, Berlin, 15 September 1959.
29 H. Scharoun, lecture delivered on the occasion of the exhibition "Berlin plant – erster Bericht", 5 September 1946, in P. Pfankuch, op. cit., p. 162.

30 The exhibition was recently reconstructed and described as an adjunct to the exhibition prepared for the 1933 CIAM Congress in Athens, see J. F. Geist, K. Kürvers, op. cit., p. 182.
31 Rudolf Pfister, 'Professor Gropius gibt gute Ratschläge', in Baumeister, vol. 44, no. 11/12, 1947, p. 389.
32 Scharoun, 'Der Raum der Mitte', in Sonntag, Berlin, 2 January 1949: 'The task of the Institute is pure research and the development of guidelines that may be applied as general principles to building as a whole. It is our concern to give new content to building practices which have lost their original creative role through everyday use.'
33 Scharoun, 'Struktur in Raum und Zeit', in Reinhard Jaspert (ed.), Handbuch moderner Architektur, Berlin 1957, p. 14.
34 Ibid. p. 17.
35 Hugo Häring,–'neues bauen', in Schriftenreihe des Bundes Deutscher Architekten, vol. 3, Hamburg 1947; quoted in Lauterbach, Joedicke, op. cit., p. 57f.
36 Scharoun, 21 June 1965, in a speech accepting an honorary doctorate from the University of Rome, in Pfankuch, op. cit., p. 139.
37 Scharoun, 'Der Raum der Mitte', op. cit.
38 Hugo Häring, 'neues bauen', op. cit., p. 57.
39 Cf. Scharoun, 'Raum und Milieu der Schule', lecture delivered at the 10th Triennale, Bauen und Wohnen, vol. 16, Munich 1961.
40 Scharoun, 'Gedanken zum Theaterraum', in Ruf zum Bauen, Berlin 1920, quoted in Pfankuch, op. cit., p. 20.
41 Scharoun, 'Das neue Staatstheater in Kassel', in Bauwelt, Berlin, no. 44, 1952, p. 173.
42 Scharoun, in the text accompanying his design for the National Theatre in Mannheim, 1953, quoted in Pfankuch, op. cit., p. 223.
43 Scharoun, manuscript of a lecture given on 15 December 1952. Scharoun Archives, Akademie der Künste, Berlin, 'The concept of intimacy provides an essential basis for controlling whether a work fulfils all the requirements of the organic or remains within the realm of geometry.'
44 Scharoun, 'Das neue Staatstheater in Kassel', op. cit., p. 177.
45 Ibid.
46 'It should be noted that the terracing of the northern half of the square shows the Classicist buildings to full advantage, confirming that this design, though conceived in a wholly new spirit, none the less shows great consideration towards the existing old buildings. The front of the Museum Fridericianum is complemented in a felicitous manner by the insertion of the new catholic church. This is conservation at its best.' Deliberations of the jury for the prize, 17–19 September 1952, Scharoun Archives, Akademie der Künste, Berlin.
47 This was part of the explanatory text for the Mannheim National Theatre, and was prepared with the help of Margot Aschenbrenner, a long-time collaborator of Hugo Häring.
48 Jean Gebser, 'Ursprung und Gegenwart': Vol. 1, Die Fundamente der aperspektivischen Welt, Beitrag zu einer Geschichte der Bewußtwerdung, Stuttgart 1949; Vol. 2, Die Manifestationen der aperspektivischen Welt, Versuch einer Konkretion des Geistigen, Stuttgart 1953. Scharoun's design for the Mannheim National Theatre dates from 1953.
49 J. Gebser, 1949, op. cit., p. 19.
50 Cf. Hugo Häring, 'Probleme der Stilbildung', in Deutsche Bauzeitung, vol. 43, 24 October 1934. In 1952 Häring also referred to Gebser. 'A Swiss scholar, Jean Gebser, has pointed out these profound changes which indicate a turning-point in our thinking. He calls this new age an a-perspectival age. However it appears to us that the concept of the a-perspective does not quite sum up what is new and different – Gebser's term contains only a technical indication of the way in which the coming age will differ from the passing one, which is characterized technically, amongst other things, by the perspective. While the term spells out one characteristic of this new age, it does not show the basis of this change.' Hugo Häring, 'vom neuen bauen', lecture, 27 May 1952, quoted in Lauterbach, Joedicke, op. cit., p. 75. For Häring this change was based on the genetic process, which he saw as clearly leading to the organic. Gebser did not share this conclusion.
51 As note 42.

52 Ibid.
53 J. Gebser, 1953, op. cit., p. 313.
54 H. Häring to Scharoun, 5 January 1953. Scharoun Archives, Akademie der Künste, Berlin.
55 'Every attempt by architects to dismantle the ramp and proscenium in order to "establish a communication between the actors and the public" is based on a misunderstanding of what the theatre is and always will be. It is pointless to invent, for the sake of a competition, a completely new kind of stage that is not required by any dramatic literature. The stage of the new Schauspielhaus should be suitable for the representation of existing dramatic literature. With the exception of the dramas of antiquity, which are presented only rarely in contemporary theatres, all this literature, including the work of the avant-garde, has been written for the proscenium stage.' Max Frisch, quoted by Hans Curjel, 'Der Zürcher Schauspielhaus-Wettbewerb', in Werk, vol. 51, no. 12, 1964, p. 439.
56 Cf. Günther Kühne, 'Die Bühne ist erfunden', in Bauwelt, no. 19, 1966, p. 533.
57 The jury for the limited competition met in October 1965. It comprised Linde, Düttmann, Kallmorgen, Fiederling, Hillebrecht and Priesing. The first prize was awarded to Scharoun, the second to Aalto. Two joint third prizes went to Spengelin and Taescher/Gerdes, and three fourth prizes to Utzon, Bornemann and Schramm/Pempelfort.
58 Cf. Stefan Wewerka, 'Scharoun entwirft', in Bau, vol. 22, no. 2, 1967, p. 37.
59 Cf. Scharoun, in collaboration with Wils Ebert, description of the Hauptstadt Berlin competition entry, quoted in Bauwelt, no. 29, 1958, p. 699.
60 Scharoun, lecture to the Friends of the Berlin Philharmonie, 27 November 1959, quoted in Pfankuch, op. cit., p. 280.
61 Scharoun, 'Struktur in Raum und Zeit', op. cit., p. 14.

Selected bibliography

Academy of Arts, Berlin, exhibition catalogues:
- *Erich Mendelsohn*, Berlin 1968
- *Hermann Muthesius*, Berlin 1978
- *Poelzig, Endell, Moll und die Breslauer Kunstakademie 1911–1932*, Berlin 1965
- *Hans Scharoun*, Berlin 1967
- *Bruno Taut 1880–1938*, Berlin 1980
- *Tendenzen der Zwanziger Jahre*, Berlin 1977

Bartning, Otto (ed.): *Darmstädter Gespräch – Mensch und Raum*, Darmstadt 1952

Behne, Adolf: *Der moderne Zweckbau*, Munich 1926

Berlinische Galerie: *Hauptstadt Berlin, Internationaler Ideenwettbewerb 1957/58,* Berlin 1990

Bürkle, J. Christoph: *Hans Scharoun und die Moderne*, Frankfurt am Main, 1986

Deutscher Werkbund (publisher): *Die Zwanziger Jahre des Deutschen Werkbundes*, Giessen 1982

Durth, Werner: *Deutsche Architekten, Biographische Verflechtungen 1900–1970*, Braunschweig/Wiesbaden 1986

Gebser, Jean: *Ursprung und Gegenwart*
- vol. 1: *Die Fundamente der aperspektivischen Welt, Beitrag zu einer Geschichte der Bewußtwerdung,* Stuttgart 1949;
- vol. 2: *Die Manifestationen der aperspektivischen Welt, Versuch einer Konkretion des Geistigen*, Stuttgart 1953

Geist, Johann Friedrich, and Kürvers, Klaus: *Das Berliner Mietshaus, 1945–1989*, vol. 3, Munich 1989

Giedion, Sigfried: *Space, Time and Architecture*, Cambridge, Mass., 1941

Graubner, Gerhard: *Theaterbau – Aufgabe und Planung*, Munich 1968

Gropius, Walter: *The Scope of Total Architecture*, London 1956

Häring, Hugo:
- *Die ausbildung des geistes zur arbeit an der gestalt, fragmente*, Schriftenreihe der Akademie der Künste, Berlin, vol. 1, Berlin 1968
- 'Neuer Struktur-Begriff', *Innen-Dekoration*, vol. 42, December 1931
- 'Form der Leistungs-Erfüllung', *Innen-Dekoration*, vol. 43, October 1932
- 'Bemerkungen zum Flachbau mit Beispielen grundsätzlicher Art', *Moderne Bauformen*, 1934
- 'Wege zu einer deutschen Baukunst', *Berliner Tageblatt*, supplement on the arts and entertainment, no. 114, 8 March 1934
- 'Das Sonnenhaus', *Das Haus*, no. 3, 1950
- 'Gespräch über die organische Baukunst', *Baukunst und Werkform*, no. 5, 1952
- 'Wege zur Form', in Lauterbach, Heinrich, and Joedicke, Jürgen: *Hugo Häring – Schriften, Bauten, Entwürfe*, Stuttgart 1965
- 'Geometrie und Organik', *Baukunst und Werkform*, September 1951
- 'Von der Seele des Wohnens', *Neuer Wohnungsbau*, edited by Hermann Wanderslebe, vol. 1, Ravensburg 1952

Heidegger, Martin:
- Being and Time (1927), New York 1962
- Vorträge und Aufsätze, Tübingen 1954
- Die Kunst und der Raum, St. Gallen 1969

Huse, Norbert (ed.): *Siedlungen der Zwanziger Jahre – heute, Vier Berliner Großsiedlungen 1924–1984*, exhibition catalogue, Berlin 1984

Janofske, Eckehard: *Architektur-Räume, Idee und Gestalt bei Hans Scharoun*, Braunschweig/Wiesbaden 1984

Jones, Peter Blundell: *Hans Scharoun: A Monograph*, London 1978

Kirsch, Karin: *Die Weissenhofsiedlung*, Stuttgart 1987

Kleihues, Josef Paul (ed.): *750 Jahre Architektur und Städtebau in Berlin, Die Internationale Bauausstellung im Kontext der Baugeschichte Berlins,* exhibition catalogue, Stuttgart 1987

Pehnt, Wolfgang: *Expressionist Architecture*, London 1973

Pfankuch, Peter (ed.):
– Hans Scharoun, *Bauten, Entwürfe, Texte*, Berlin 1974
– Adolf Rading, *Bauten, Entwürfe und Erläuterungen*, Berlin 1970

Posener, Julius:
– *Anfänge des Funktionalismus*, Berlin/Frankfurt am Main/Vienna 1964
– *Aufsätze und Vorträge 1931–1980*, Braunschweig 1981
– 'Vorlesungen zur Geschichte der Neuen Architektur', 1–3, *Arch+*, Aachen 1979, 1980, 1981

Reichow, Hans Bernhard: *Organische Baukunst*, Braunschweig 1949

Scarpa, Ludovica: *Martin Wagner und Berlin*, Braunschweig/Wiesbaden 1986

Scharoun, Hans:
– 'Gedanken zur neuen Gestalt der Stadt', *Bildende Kunst*, Berlin, vol. 1, no. 6, 1947
– 'Wohnhaus der Zukunft', *Sonntag*, Berlin, 3 July 1949
– 'Der Raum der Mitte', *Sonntag,* Berlin, 2 January 1949
– 'Zur Situation des Städtebaus und der Städtebaulehre', *Die T.U.*, Berlin, vol. 5, nos. 2/3, 1949
– Explanatory text on the Darmstadt elementary school, *Darmstädter Gespräch 1951*, Darmstadt 1952
– 'Phantasie und geistige Ordnung – aus Aufsätzen Hugo Härings', *Die neue Stadt*, Darmstadt, vol. 6, no. 5, 1952
– 'Das neue Staatstheater in Kassel', *Bauwelt*, Berlin, no. 44, 1952
– 'Vom Stadt-Wesen und Architekt-Sein', acceptance speech for Fritz Schumacher Prize, *Gedenkschrift zur Verleihung des Fritz-Schumacher-Preises 1954*, Hamburg
– 'Zur Frage des "Neues Bauens"', *Lebendige Kunst, Beilage zu Pädagogische Blätter,* Berlin, nos. 5/6, 1954
– *Medizin und Städtebau*, edited by Paul Vogeler and Erich Kühn, Munich/Berlin/Vienna 1957
– 'Struktur in Raum und Zeit', in *Handbuch moderner Architektur*, by Reinhard Jaspert (ed.), Berlin 1957
– 'Vom Wesen der Stadt', *Der Tagesspiegel*, Berlin, 15 September 1949, reprinted in *Der Architekt*, Essen, vol. 12, no. 10, 1963
– 'Raum für die Muße', *Deutsche Zeitung*, Cologne, 21 May 1961
– 'Raum und Milieu der Schule', lecture at the XI Triennale of *Bauen+Wohnen*, Munich, vol. 16, no. 4, 1961
– 'Struktur und Gestalt', *Veröffentlichungen des Zentralinstituts für Städtebau der Technischen Universität Berlin*, 1962
– 'Musik im Mittelpunkt', *Philharmonische Blätter*, Berlin, no. 13, 1963; reprinted in *Der Architekt*, no. 10, 1964
– 'Zur Ausstellung "Berlin plant"', Neue Bauwelt, Berlin, vol. 2, no. 37, 1947
– 'Baukunst: Sinngebung des Lebens', extract from Scharoun's acceptance speech on being awarded an honorary doctorate by the University of Rome, *Bauwelt*, Berlin, vol. 56, no. 28, 1965
– *Praemium Erasmianum MCMLXX*, commemorative journal, Amsterdam 1970; acceptance speech for the Prize, foreword in Lauterbach, Heinrich: *Bauten*, Berlin 1971

Staber, Margit: 'Hans Scharoun, ein Beitrag zum Organischen Bauen', *Zodiac 10,* Milan 1962 (with English translation)

Vesper, Ekkehart (ed.): *Staatsbibliothek Preußischer Kulturbesitz*, commemorative journal to mark the opening of the State Library in Berlin, Wiesbaden 1978

List of works

1. Church in Bremerhaven, 1911. Competition designs: 'Everything for Love' and 'Andante'.
2. Building on the Kaiser-Wilhelm-Platz in Geestemünde, 1913. 'Erlebtes' competition entry.
3. Kruchen House, Buch, near Berlin, 1913. With Paul Kruchen.
4. Freymuth Sanatorium, Babelsberg, near Berlin, 1913. With Paul Kruchen.
5. Grunewald Sanatorium, Grunewald, near Berlin, 1913. With Paul Kruchen. Project.
6. Mariendorf Hospital, near Berlin, 1914. With Paul Kruchen.
7. Circular house, Angerburg, 1914. 'Preußen' competition entry.
8. Development plans for a district in Gumbinnen, East Prussia, 1915. Unbuilt design.
9. Temporary church, Walterkehmen, East Prussia, 1916. Conversion of a riding arena in an estate.
10. Guest house by the Goldapersee, East Prussia, 1916. Unbuilt design.
11. Community centre, Kattenau, East Prussia, 1917.
12. Manor house, Thierfeld, near Gumbinnen, East Prussia, 1917/18.
13. Housing near Insterburg, East Prussia, 1918. Semi-detached houses with stables.
14. Small houses for the white-colour housing association (Beamten-Wohnungsbau-Gesellschaft) of Insterburg, East Prussia, 1919. Detached, semi-detached, terrace and four-family houses. Project.
15. Tivoli, Insterburg, East Prussia, 1919. Conversion of festival hall into a theatre. Project.
16. Cemetery for the city of Dortmund, 1919. 'Erhebung' competition entry.
17. Development plan for the cathedral square of Prenzlau, 1919. First prize in 'Vorhof' competition.
18. Emmerich Town Hall, c. 1919. 'Virgo' competition entry.
19. Prenzlau swimming pool, c. 1919. 'Licht' competition entry.
20. 'Pregelstraße' semi-detached house, Insterburg, East Prussia, 1920.
21. Gutzeit House, near Gumbinnen, East Prussia, 1920. Conversion.
22. Kamswyken housing, near Insterburg, East Prussia, 'Die bunte Reihe', 1920.
23. Theatre, social and cultural hall, Gelsenkirchen, 1920. 'Der Mensch ist gut' competition entry.
24. Extension of shop and storage facilities for the firm of Matheus Müller in Eltville, Rhein-Hessen, 1920. 'Bei einer Flasche M. M.' competition entry.
25. Town hall and church square in Lyck, East Prussia, 1920. 'KIK' competition entry.
26. City expansion plan, Insterburg, East Prussia, 1920/21. Competition entry.
27. Post office in Bremen station, 1921. 'Betrieb nicht Repräsentation' competition entry.
28. Dresden Museum of Hygiene, 1920. 'Kultur und Zivilisation' competition entry.
29. Development of a new market in Insterburg, East Prussia. Competition entry, first prize.
30. Albat manor house, Santilten, East Prussia, 1921/22. Conversion.
31. Zimmermann estate, smithy and stables, Kuinen, East Prussia, 1922.
32. Commercial building at the Börsenhof, Königsberg, East Prussia, 1922. 'Zeittakt' competition entry.
33. Chicago Tribune Tower, 1922. Competition entry.
34. Friedrichstraße high-rise, Berlin, 1922. 'Innen und Außen' competition entry. Commendation.
35. Pluquet grain store, Wertheim, East Prussia, 1922.
36. Wesel town hall, 1922. Competition entry.
37. Single-family house on the Ufergasse, Insterburg, East Prussia, 1922.
38. Gobert semi-detached house, Sodehnen, East Prussia, 1922.
39. Memorial to Kant, Königsberg, East Prussia, 1922. Competition entry.
40. Voss residential and commercial building, Ziegelstraße 1, Insterburg, East Prussia, 1922. Conversion.
41. Three- and four-storey apartment houses on the Parkring, Insterburg, East Prussia, 1923/24.
42. Development of the Prinz Albrecht Gardens, Berlin, 1924. 'Ho Tro' (Hoffmanns Tropfen) competition entry.

43 Ulm cathedral square, 1924/25. 'Umfassen und Scheiden' competition entry.
44 Spa building, Bad Mergentheim, Württemberg, 1924/25. 'Schweben' competition entry.
45 Commercial building in Frankfurt a. d. Oder, 1924/25. 'Vitrine der Industrie' competition entry.
46 House for Professor Siegel, Insterburg, East Prussia, 1925. Project.
47 Tannenberg memorial, 1925. 'Spiel mit der Landschaft' competition entry.
48 Bochum town hall, 1925. 'Kopf und Bauch der Stadt' competition entry.
49 Konitzer department store, Marienburg, East Prussia, 1925. Project.
50 Water tower, c. 1925. Three versions, competition entry.
51 Cologne bridgehead, 1925. 'Zwischen Brücke und Dom' competition entry. Commendation.
52 Trade fair and exhibition centre, Berlin, 1927. 'Spinne' competition entry.
53 Square in front of Duisburg station, 1926. 'Vorschlag 3' competition entry.
54 The elastic groundplan, 1926. Variable types for multi-storey housing.
55 Pöpelwitz *Siedlung*, Breslau, 1926. 'Wohneinheit' competition entry. Commendation.
56 Town hall, Insterburg, East Prussia, 1927. 'Grüße' competition entry.
57 Breslau exhibition centre, 1927. Project, two versions.
58 Transportable wooden house for the German Garden and Trades Exhibition, Liegnitz, 1927. Manufactured by Christoph & Unmack, Niesky.
59 Single-family home for the Werkbund Exhibition, 'Die Wohnung', Weissenhof, Stuttgart, from 23 July to 23 October 1927.
60 Road through the Ministry Gardens, Berlin, 1927. Urban planning proposal.
61 Fire station and administrative building, Breslau, 1927. Competition entry.
62 Extension of the Reichstag, Berlin, 1927. 'Balance' competition entry, 2 versions.
63 Adriabad, swimming pool at the Zoo, Berlin, 1927. Unbuilt design.
64 Dahlem-Dorf housing, Berlin, 1927. Unbuilt design.
65 Protestant church, Breslau-Zimpel, 1932. Competition entry.
66 School, Breslau-Zimpel, 1928. Competition entry.
67 Housing for single people, 1928. Preliminary design for the Werkbund exhibition in Breslau, 1929.
68 City hall and exhibition centre, Bremen, 1928. 'Bremer Flagge' competition entry. Commendation.
69 Schlichtallee group of schools, Berlin-Lichtenberg, 1928. 'Entwicklung' competition entry.
70 Single-family house, 1928. 'Weite' competition entry for Velhagen & Klasings monthly journal.
71 Hotel in Wesermünde, 1928. Project.
72 Memorial to Richard Wagner, Leipzig, c. 1928. Competition entry.
73 Apartment building at Kaiserdamm 25, at the corner of Königin-Elisabeth-Straße and Fredericiastraße, Berlin-Charlottenburg, 1928/29.
74 Housing on the Kaiserstraße, Bremerhaven, 1929.
75 Housing on the Heidelberger Platz, Berlin-Wilmersdorf, 1929. Project.
76 Housing block at Paulsborner/Eisenzahn-/Westfälische-/Albrecht-Achilles-Straße, Berlin-Wilmersdorf, 1929. Unbuilt design.
77 Housing block for the Werkbund Exhibition 'Wohnung und Werkraum', Breslau, from 15 June to 15 September 1929.
78 Exhibition for Desta, German Iron and Steel Corporation, 1929. Project.
79 Apartment building at Hohenzollerndamm 35/36 and Mansfelder Straße 29, Berlin-Wilmersdorf, 1929/30.
80 Berlin law courts, Invalidenstraße, Alt-Moabit, Rathenower Straße, Berlin-Tiergarten, 1930. Competition entry.
81 Siemensstadt *Siedlung*, Berlin 1930. Planning and housing on the Jungfernheideweg and Mäckeritzstraße. Landscaping: Leberecht Migge.
82 Lindner housing block, Berlin 1930. Project.
83 Terrace housing, Schlachtensee type, 1930. Project.
84 Terrace housing, Halensee type, 1930. Project.
85 Memorial to Richard Wagner, Leipzig, c. 1930. Competition entry.
86 Housing at Flinsberger Platz 3, Berlin-Wilmersdorf, 1931.

87 Rostock city hall, 1930. Competition entry.
88 House front advertisement for Leiser, Berlin, 1931. Not realized.
89 War memorial in Thüringer Wald, 1931. 'Erdmal' competition entry.
90 Steinhausen house, Falkenhain, near Berlin, 1931. Conversion project.
91 The contemporary private house, 1931. 'Bauwelt' magazine competition entry.
92 Housing at Kottbusser Tor, Berlin-Kreuzberg, 1931. Project.
93 Housing at Treseburger Ufer, Berlin-Neukölln, 1931. Unbuilt design.
94 Housing on the Hauptstraße, Berlin-Schöneberg, 1931. Project.
95 Housing on the Kaiserdamm, Berlin-Charlottenburg, 1931. Project.
96 Wonolett, 1931. Prototype ground-plan. Unrealized.
97 Three single-family houses for Ferdinand Möller, Potsdam, 1931. Unrealized.
98 Pergola house, Berlin, 1931. Project.
99 Single-family house, Löbau type, 1931. Project.
100 Single-family double house, 1931. Linked houses on a slope. Design.
101 Social housing on the edge of the city, 1931. Project, with Erwin Gutkind.
102 Housing block and cinema, Spandauer Damm at the corner of Sophie-Charlotten-Straße, Berlin-Charlottenburg, 1931. Project.
103 Berlin resettlement, 1931. Two-storey terraces of apartments. Project.
104 Typical ground-plans for four-storey housing, 1931. Unrealized.
105 Wannsee housing development, Berlin-Wannsee, 1931. Project.
106 Reichsstraße apartment building, Berlin-Charlottenburg, 1931. Project.
107 Apartment types for a building with a central passage, 1931. Project.
108 Hindenburgplatz apartment building, Bremerhaven, 1931. Project.
109 Single-family house, 1932. Flat-roofed types I, II, III. Unrealized.
110 Building module, 1932. Typical ground-plans. Unrealized.
111 'Growing house' for the 'Sun, Air and Housing for Everyone' Exhibition, Berlin, 1932.
112 Housing block, Landsberger Allee, Berlin-Lichtenberg, 1932. Project.
113 Cinema in Bremerhaven, 1932. Project.
114 Panke Park, park running from Berlin-Wedding to Bernau, 1932. Project.
115 The transportable house, 1932. Typical ground-plans. Unrealized.
116 Housing block on the Hohenzollernring, Berlin-Spandau, 1932.
117 Wenzeck house, Berlin-Frohnau, 1932.
118 Schuldenfrey House, Garystraße 26, Berlin-Dahlem, 1932.
119 Housing block with variable accommodation, 1932. Project.
120 Housing block, 1932. One- and two-bed type, four and six storeys. Project.
121 Single-family home with summer house, 1932. Project.
122 Housing block, Zweibrücker Straße 38–46, Berlin-Spandau, 1933.
123 The variable dwelling, housing for single people and others, 1933. Unrealized.
124 Schminke house, Löbau, Saxony, 1933. Garden design: Herta Hammerbacher.
125 Strauß House, Hüninger Straße, Berlin-Dahlem, 1933.
126 Redevelopment of the Normalm quarter of Stockholm, 1933. Competition entry.
127 Housing on the Alexanderplatz, Berlin, 1933. Project.
128 Mattern House, Bornim, near Potsdam, 1933. Garden design: Hermann Mattern.
129 Anker pasta factory, Loeser & Richter, garage, canteen, premises conversion, Löbau, Saxony, 1934.
130 Nordsee group of single-family houses at the Bürgerpark, Wesermünde, c. 1934. Project.
131 Holiday apartments for a hotel in Vitznau, Switzerland, 1934. Project.
132 Shop for the Müller-Örlinghausen mosaic workshop, Clausewitzstraße, Berlin-Charlottenburg, 1934.
133 House for Professor Gocht, 1934. Project.
134 Baensch house, Weinmeisterhöhe, Höhenweg 9, Berlin-Spandau, 1935. Garden design: Hermann Mattern.
135 Hoffmeyer house, Friesenstraße 6, Bremerhaven, 1935.
136 Small and medium-sized houses, Kladow-Hottengrund, Berlin, 1933.

137 Pflaum house, Falkensee, near Berlin, 1935. Garden design: Hermann Mattern.
138 Housing at Kaiserstraße 224–238, Bremerhaven, 1936.
139 Im Eichengrund housing, Berlin-Heiligensee, 1936.
140 Oskar Moll house, Berlin-Grunewald, 1936. Garden design: Hermann Mattern. Destroyed in 1944.
141 Single-family houses on the Elbestraße, Bremerhaven, 1937.
142 Ferdinand Möller house, Zermützelsee, near Altruppin, Mark Brandenburg, 1937. Garden design: Hermann Mattern.
143 Biskupski house, Zermützelsee, near Altruppin, Mark Brandenburg, 1938.
144 Single-family houses on the Bleßmannstraße, Bremerhaven, 1938.
145 Wolfgang Krüger house, An der Rehwiese 4, Berlin-Nikolassee, 1938. Conversion.
146 Bonk house, Bornim, near Potsdam, 1938.
147 Single-family houses on the Humboldtstraße, Berlin-Reinickendorf, 1938. Project.
148 Single-family house for Hilde Just, Berlin-Schlachtensee, 1938. Project.
149 Noack house, near Potsdam, 1937/38.
150 Residential building for eight families, Yorkstraße, Bremerhaven, 1938. Conversion project.
151 Weidhaas house, Leipzig, 1939. Project, two versions.
152 Silbermann garden bath-house, Brandenburg, Havel, 1939.
153 Scharf house, Miquelstraße 39a and b, Berlin-Schmargendorf, 1939. Garden design: Hermann Mattern.
154 Mohrmann house, Falkensteinstraße 10, Berlin-Lichtenrade, 1939. Garden design: Hermann Mattern.
155 Housing at Kaiserstraße 240–254, Bremerhaven, 1940.
156 Fritz Endell house, Am kleinen Wannsee 30b, Berlin-Wannsee, 1940.
157 Studio conversion, Kantstraße 12, Berlin-Charlottenburg, c. 1940.
158 Central laundry facilities, research work, 1941–1943.
159 Otto Weigand house, Borgsdorf, near Berlin, 1942.
160 Müller-Örlinghausen house, Kreßbronn, Bodensee, 1943. Conversion.
161 Extension to Ferdinand Möller house, Zermützelsee, near Altruppin, Mark Brandenburg, 1943.
162 'Berlin plans – a first report'. Planning for the reconstruction of Berlin, exhibition in the White Hall of Berlin Castle, 1946. With a planning collective comprised of: Wils Ebert, Peter Friedrich, Ludmilla Herzenstein, Reinhold Lingner, Louise Seitz, Selman Selmanagic, Herbert Weinberger.
163 House of synthetic materials, 'German type', 1946. With Karl Böttcher. Design and model house.
164 Exhibition centre at the Friedrichstraße station, Berlin, 1946. Project.
165 Wilhelm house, Berlin-Kladow, 1948. Project.
166 America house, Bremerhaven, 1946. Conversion.
167 Exhibition pavilion for the Gerd Rosen gallery, Berlin, 1948. Project.
168 Leipzig opera house, 1949. Competition entry.
169 Magdeburg cellulose factory, Rothensee, 1949. Project.
170 Friedrichshain neighbourhood, Berlin, 1949. Unrealized site plan and buildings.
171 Stuttgart Music Hall, 1949. Competition entry, first prize.
172 Conversion of the Institute of Building Science, German Academy of Science, Hannoversche Straße 30, Berlin, 1949.
173 Schminke house, Celle, 1950. Project.
174 Residential and commercial building, Kurfürstendamm 182 at the corner of Olivaer Platz, Berlin-Charlottenburg, 1950. Project.
175 Darmstadt elementary school, 1951. Project.
176 America Memorial Library, Blücherplatz, Berlin-Kreuzberg, 1951. Competition entry, second prize.
177 Heinrich Mendelsohn high-rise on the Lietzensee, Kaiserdamm/Sophie-Charlotten-Straße/Wundtstraße, Berlin-Charlottenburg, 1952. Competition entry.
178 Siemensstadt centre, Jungfernheideweg at the corner of Siemensdamm, Berlin, c. 1952. Project.
179 High-rise housing for the Siemensstadt *Siedlung*, Jungfernheideweg at the corner of Siemensdamm, Berlin, 1952. Project.
180 Kassel State Theatre, 1952. Competition entry, first prize. With Hermann Mattern and Willem Huller.
181 Kassel State Theatre, 1953/54. Working drawings. With Hermann Mattern.

182 Old people's home, Lehrter Straße, Berlin-Tiergarten, 1952. Competition entry, first prize.
183 Helgoland, 1952. Competition entry. Commendation.
184 Helgoland, sample houses, 1953. Unbuilt design.
185 National Theatre, Mannheim, 1953. Competition design.
186 Gelsenkirchen Theatre, 1954. Competition design.
187 'Romeo and Juliet' high-rises, Stuttgart-Zuffenhausen, 1954–1959. With Wilhelm Frank.
188 School for the Friedrich Ebert Foundation, Bergneustadt, 1955. Competition entry.
189 Office building for the Hannoversche Lebensversicherung insurance company, Hanover, 1954/55. Competition entry.
190 Hamburg market hall, Hammerbrook, 1955. Competition entry.
191 Development proposal for Marl, Westphalia, 1955.
192 Restaurant in the Hansa district, Berlin-Tiergarten, 1955. Project.
193 Administrative building for the Wella company, Darmstadt, 1955. Competition entry, two versions.
194 Stroeher house, Darmstadt, 1955. Project, with Chen Kuan Lee.
195 Addition to Otto Bartning's housing on Goebelstraße 1–9, Berlin-Siemensstadt, 1955.
196 Charlottenburg-Nord *Siedlung*, Berlin, 1956–1961. Site plan and housing blocks at Heilmannring and Goebelplatz.
197 Bürgerweide, Bremen, 1956. Urban planning competition, first prize.
198 Nursing home, Stuttgart-Botnang, 1956. Project.
199 Krupp nurses' home, Essen, 1956. Competition entry.
200 Development plan of the Hansa district, Berlin-Tiergarten, 1956. Project.
201 Single-family homes in the Hansa district, Berlin-Tiergarten, 1956. Project.
202 Concert hall for the Berlin Philharmonic Orchestra, Bundesallee 1, Berlin-Wilmersdorf, 1956. Competition entry, first prize.
203 School centre at Holterhöfchen, Hilden, Westphalia, 1957. Competition entry.
204 The 'Geschwister Scholl' School, Lünen, Westphalia, 1956–1962.
205 Bremen city hall, 1957. Competition entry.
206 Saarbrücken concert hall, 1958. Competition entry, third prize.
207 Goebelplatz shopping centre, Berlin-Charlottenburg-Nord, 1957. Project.
208 Spandau old town, Berlin, 1958. Urban planning sketches.
209 Von Rothenburg house, Berlin-Dahlem, 1958. Conversion project.
210 Städtische Sparkasse (Savings Bank), Stuttgart, 1958. Proposal.
211 Town hall, Marl, Westphalia, 1958. Competition entry, second prize.
212 'Hauptstadt Berlin' competition, 1958. Second prize, with Wils Ebert.
213 'Der fröhliche Bierberg', Reeperbahn-Millerntor, Hamburg, 1959. Urban planning report.
214 School in Marl, Westphalia, 1961.
215 Designs for studio apartments, Berlin, 1960.
216 College for social sciences, Linz, Austria, 1961. Competition design.
217 'Salute' high-rise, Stuttgart, 1961–1963. With Wilhelm Frank.
218 Housing for foreign aid workers, Stuttgart, 1962. Project.
219 'Leere Vasen' housing blocks, Böblingen, near Stuttgart, 1962. Project.
220 DuMont Schauberg publishing house, Cologne, 1962. Project.
221 Development proposal for the area around the cathedral and Römerberg, Frankfurt, 1963. Competition entry, third prize.
222 Concert hall for the Berlin Philharmonic Orchestra, Kemperplatz, Berlin-Tiergarten, 1963. With Werner Weber. Landscape design: Hermann Mattern.
223 Development plan for the Mehringplatz, Berlin-Kreuzberg, 1963. Competition entry, first prize.
224 Neven-DuMont single-family house, Cologne, 1964. Project.
225 Pforzheim city hall, 1964. Competition entry.
226 Zurich Schauspielhaus, 1964. Competition entry.
227 BP office building, Hamburg, 1964. Competition entry. Commendation.

228 State Library for the Prussian Cultural Heritage Foundation, Berlin-Tiergarten, 1964. Competition design, first prize.
229 Municipal Theatre, Wolfsburg, 1965. Competition entry, first prize.
230 'Rauhe Kapf' residential neighbourhood, Böblingen, near Stuttgart, 1965.
231 House for Dr Tormann, Bad Homburg v. d. Höhe, 1966.
232 Institute of the Faculty of Architecture, Technische Universität of Berlin, 1966. With Bernhard Hermkes.
233 Chapel of St. John for the Community of Christ in Glockengarten, Bochum, 1966. With Gundolf Bockemühl.
234 Church of the Transfiguration of Christ, Viktoria-Luise-Platz, Berlin-Schöneberg, 1966. Project.
235 Society of Art and guest house, Matthäikirchplatz, 1966. Project.
236 State Library for the Prussian Cultural Heritage Foundation, 1963/64. With Edgar Wisniewski. Consultant: Hermann Fehling. Landscape design: Hermann Mattern, Günther Nagel.
237 Rot car salesroom, Stuttgart-Zuffenhausen, 1968.
238 Köpke house, Im Dol 10, Berlin-Dahlem, 1968.
239 Hasenbergsteige housing blocks, Stuttgart, 1969. Project.
240 Protestant church and community centre, Wolfsburg-Rabenberg, 1970.
241 Kindergarten, Wolfsburg-Detmerode, 1970.
242 High-rise housing at Zabel-Krüger-Damm, Berlin-Reinickendorf, 1970.
243 AOK Headquarters, Mehringplatz, Berlin-Kreuzberg, 1970. With Bodo Fleischer.
244 German Maritime Museum, Bremerhaven, 1970–1977. Project architect: Peter Fromlowitz, with Helmut Bohnsack.
245 'Orplid' high-rise, Böblingen, 1971.
246 Chamber Music Hall for the Philharmonic Orchestra, Kemperplatz, Berlin-Tiergarten, 1971. Work cooperative Scharoun-Wisniewski.
247 State Institute for Musical Research and Museum of Instruments, Berlin-Tiergarten, 1971. Work cooperative Scharoun-Wisniewski.
249 German Embassy in Brasilia, 1971. Project architect: Fried Schnabel.
250 Municipal Theatre, Wolfsburg, 1973. Project architect: Peter-Fritz Hoffmeyer, with the engineering practice of Friese und Bendorf.

Illustration credits

We would like to thank the Akademie der Künste in Berlin for making available documents and extensive photographic material, and in particular Frau Ursula Reich, Dr Matthias Schirren and Achim Wendschuh for their kind assistance and cooperation.

Buderus Aktiengesellschaft, Wetzlar: 115 above
Bundesbaudirektion, Berlin: 140, 141 above and middle
Friedrich Reinhard, Berlin: Cover front, 125 below, 126/27, 129 below, 139 above and below, 144 below, 149 above, 153 middle and below, 155, 156/57
Hagemann, Otto, Berlin: 79
Köves, Ivan, Marl: 133 below
Lossen & Co., Stuttgart: 63 below
Minzloff, Hans L., Berlin: 113 below
Planck, Gottfried, Stuttgart: 135
Storp, Dieter, Düsseldorf: 129 above

All other illustrations: Akademie der Künste, Berlin, and author.

TechArt created this comp for Bay Meadows race track by scanning a photograph, which printed cleanly and sharply on the company's laser printer and gave the client a clear idea of what the finished product would look like.